HOW TO UNDERSTAND
AND
MASTER SECURITIES LAWS
& REGULATIONS

A Manual for Series 66 Success

Created & Developed By:

THOMAS ANTHONY GUERRIERO

Order this book online at www.trafford.com
or email orders@trafford.com

Most Trafford titles are also available at major online book retailers.

Printed in the United States of America.

ISBN: 978-1-4669-5489-2 (sc)
ISBN: 978-1-4669-5490-8 (e)

Trafford rev. 08/28/2012

 www.trafford.com

North America & international
toll-free: 1 888 232 4444 (USA & Canada)
phone: 250 383 6864 ♦ fax: 812 355 4082

Table of Contents

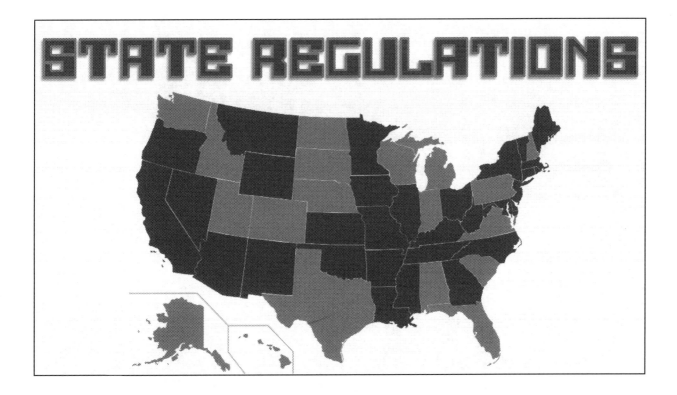

Definitions

Administrator: The office or agency responsible for administering the securities laws of the state. The Administrator has jurisdiction over all securities activity, and the registration of securities and securities professionals. The Administrator is also responsible for making rules and issuing orders.

The Administrator has to power to conduct investigations, publish information about violations, subpoena persons and records, compel testimony that incriminates, issue a cease and desist order without providing a hearing

Definitions

Persons:
Individuals (human beings), Corporations, Partnerships, Business Trusts, Estates, Trusts, Associations, Joint Stock Companies or Joint Ventures, Governments and Political Subdivisions of Governments, and Unincorporated Organizations and any other legal or commercial entity

A person may issue or trade securities

Issuer:
Any person who issues, or proposes to issue, securities.

Issuer Transaction
When an issuer sells or redeems securities. The sale of the securities is for the benefit of the issuer (Primary Transaction)

Issuer For Trusts
For securities where the structure is such that there is no Board of Directors. The issuer is defined as the person performing the functions of manager or depositor under the Trust agreement

Issuer for Equipment Trusts
The trust is the person to whom the equipment is to be leased or conditionally sold

Uniform Securities Act (USA)

The USA was drafted in response to the need for uniformity between the securities laws passed by individual states. The USA is not actual legislation, it is a model that each state uses to draft securities laws. Most states follow the USA very closely.

State Blue Sky Laws

State registration laws. These laws pre-date the adoption of the Federal Securities Acts of 1933 and 1934. Larger states passed securities laws to protect their citizens from fraud

An Investment Adviser is defined as a person that:

- Engages in the business of advising others, directly or indirectly, as to the value of securities or the advisability of investing, buying, or selling securities
- Issues or promulgates analyses or reports concerning securities on a regular basis as part of a business
- Provides investment advisory services to others in a financial planning practice

Investment Advisers

The following are NOT defined as investment advisers:

- Employees of investment advisers (investment adviser representatives)
- Depository Institutions (banks, savings and loans, trusts)
- Professionals (lawyers, accountants, engineers, teachers)
- Broker-dealers whose performance of these services is incidental to the conduct of the business and who receive no special compensation for these services
- Publishers, employees or columnists of bona-fide newspapers, news magazines, business or financial periodicals and owners and employees of cable radio, or televisions networks, where the content does NOT consist of rendering advice based upon specific investment situation of each client
- Federal Covered Advisers

Federal Covered Advisers

Federal Covered Advisers are defined as:

- Investment advisers that manage $25 million or more of assets
- Investment advisers to registered investment companies

The following must register with the SEC:

- Nationally recognized statistical ratings organizations (Moody's or Standard & Poor's)
- Newly formed advisers that reasonably expect to have at least $25 million of assets under management within 120 days of formation
- A State registered adviser that is an affiliate of an SEC registered adviser
- An adviser that is required to be registered in 30 or more states

Investment Adviser Representatives are defined as:

- Any partner, officer, director, or other individual employed by an investment adviser who:
- Makes recommendations or renders advice regarding securities
- Manages accounts or portfolios of clients
- Determines which recommendations or advice regarding securities should be given
- Solicits, offers, or negotiates for the sale of investment advisory services
- Supervises employees who perform any of the functions listed above

*Employees who solely perform clerical or ministerial duties are excluded from the definition of an investment adviser representative

Registration/Notice Requirements for Investment Advisers

An individual must register as an investment adviser in order to transact business in that state, unless that individual is exempt from licensing

An individual must be registered as an investment adviser representative in the state to be employed by an investment adviser

Investment advisers must promptly notify the Administrator upon the beginning or termination of a representative

Investment advisers are prohibited from employing any person has been suspended or barred by the Administrator from association with a broker-dealer or investment adviser

Broker-Dealer
A person who engages in the business of effecting securities transactions for the account of others or his own account. Broker-Dealers must register with any state in which they solicit or conduct business

Agency Capacity
When a firm performs a transactions for the account of others. In this instance the firm is a "broker"

Principal Capacity
When a firm trades for its own account. The firm is considered to be a "dealer"

Persons NOT considered to be broker-dealers

- Banks, Savings Institutions, and Trust Companies, and Issuers
- Firms that trade exclusively with professional investors with no place of business in that State
- Firms that contact existing customers on vacation in another state (firms that are licensed in one state that contact an existing customer vacationing in a state in which the firm is not registered)
- Canadian broker-dealers
- Persons with no office in the state with a maximum of 5 clients in the past 12 months

Agent
(sales representative)

- An individual who represents a broker-dealer and effects trades
- May be compensated on commission or salary basis

- Broker-dealer employees who do not effect trades are not agents
- Individuals representing issuers in exempted transactions or transactions of exempted securities are not agents
- Individuals who represent issuers in effecting trades in "covered" securities
- Employees of an issuer who only effect trades for the issuer's employees

Registration Requirements for Broker-Dealers and Agents

- It is unlawful for any person to transact business as a broker-dealer organization unless that person is registered in the State
- Broker-dealers are prohibited from employing an agent unless the agent is registered. An agent's registration ceases to be effective in the State once he is no longer employed by the broker-dealer
- Agents are prohibited from being associated with more than one broker-dealer unless the broker-dealers are affiliated (some states do allow dual registration)
- Agents can only register through a broker-dealer. If a broker-dealer loses its registration, its agents are no longer registered wit that firm. The agents may associate with another firm

Exemptions

- Broker-dealers that have no place of business in a State or with 5 or fewer clients in that State in a 12-month period
- Canadian broker-dealers with no place of business in a State, whose customers are temporarily visiting that State
- Agents associated with exempt broker-dealers are exempt
- Individuals who do not fall under the definition of an "agent"

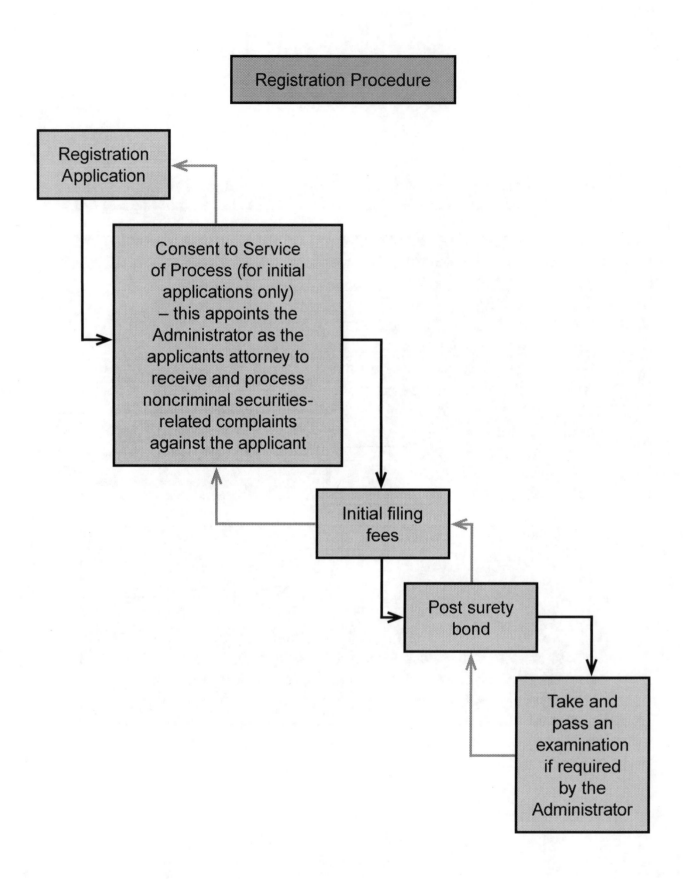

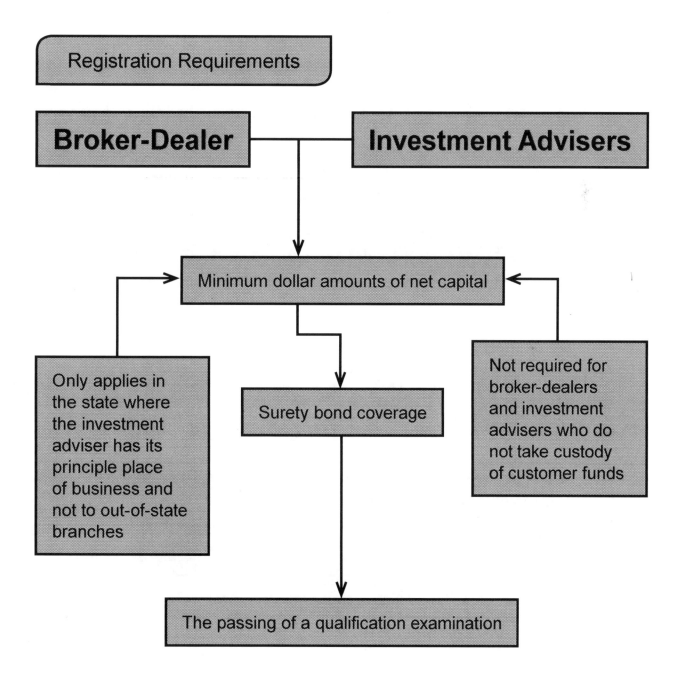

Registration Requirements

Broker-Dealer   **Investment Advisers**

Minimum dollar amounts of net capital

Only applies in the state where the investment adviser has its principle place of business and not to out-of-state branches

Surety bond coverage

Not required for broker-dealers and investment advisers who do not take custody of customer funds

The passing of a qualification examination

NATIONAL SECURITIES MARKETS IMPROVEMENT ACT

Passed in 1996, this federal law was passed to eliminate duplicate regulations that required registration at both the Federal and State level

If registration is required at the Federal level, the State cannot require registration

If registration is not required at the Federal Level, the State can require registration

Federal law supersedes state laws regarding net capital rules, custody rules, margin rules, financial responsibility rules and recordkeeping rules

Securities

A security is an investment in a common enterprise for profit, with management performed by another party

Corporate securities

- Common and preferred stock
- Notes, Bonds, Debentures
- Treasury stock
- Collateral Trust Certificates
- Equipment Trust Certificates
- Real Estate Investment Trusts
- American Depository Receipts
- Collateral Mortgage Obligations
- Rights and Warrants
- Voting Trust Certificates

Investment Company Securities

- Open End Fund Shares (mutual funds)
- Closed End Fund Shares
- Investment Contracts
- Unit Investment Trusts
- Variable Annuity Contracts

Government Securities

- US Government Obligations
- Government Agency Obligations
- Obligations of States and Political Subdivisions
- Foreign Government Obligations

Securities

Options Contracts

Options Contracts on stocks, debt instruments , indexes and foreign currency

Tax Sheltered Securities

Pre-organized certificates
Certificates of interest in a Profit Sharing Arrangement
Fractional interests in oil, gas, or mining ventures
Real Estate Condominiums
Farming, planting and breeding programs

Other Securities

Whiskey Warehouse Receipts
Merchandising Marketing Schemes
Commodity Options Contracts

Issues not defined as securities

Insurance or Endowment Policies or Contracts
Fixed Annuity Contracts
Commodities Futures Contracts
Interests in both contributory and non-contributory retirement plans

Exempt Securities
Securities issued by:
- U.S. Government
- Foreign Governments
- Municipal Governments
- Canadian Governments
- Bank and Savings Institutions
- Trust Companies

Exempt Transactions
- Isolated transactions with someone other than an issuer
- Transactions between issuers and underwriters
- Transactions with financial or institutional investors (these transactions are exempt because the investors involved are sophisticated and are not deemed to require legislative protection

Covered Transactions
- Private placement
- Sales to qualified purchasers
  - Natural persons or family owned companies with investments of at least $5 million
  - Pre-existing trusts for the persons listed above as qualified purchasers
- Any other person, acting for its own account or for other qualified purchasers, who owns and invests on a discretionary basis, at least $25 million

Registration of Securities

Any security being offered or sold in a state must be registered under the Act or as a federal covered security

Each registration is effective for 1 year. During that year, the Administrator can require quarterly reports on the progress of the offering

The State can require filing of any advertising and sales literature, prospectuses, circulars or form letters used in connection with the offering

Types of Registrations

Registration by Coordination

Registration by coordination is filed with the state if the company has already filed a registration statement under the Securities Act of 1933 Issuers must supply the following records:

- Copies of the latest form of prospectus filed under the Securities Act of 1933, if the Administrator requires it
- A copy of the company's articles of incorporation and bylaws, a copy of the underwriting agreement or a sample copy of the security

Effective Date

- Registration by coordination becomes effective on the same day as the federal registration becomes effective if:
- No stop orders were issued by the Administrator
- The registration has been file for at least 10 or 20 days depending on the state
- A statement of the maximum and minimum offering prices and underwriting discounts have been on file for two business days

Types of Registrations

Registration by Qualification

Securities that are not eligible by another method and securities that will be sold only in one state will be registered by qualification. The information needed by the issuer is as follows:

- Name, address, form of organization, description of property, and type of business
- Information on directors and officers and every owner of 10% or more of the issuers securities, and the remuneration paid to owners in the last 12 months
- Description of issuers' capitalization and long-term debt
- Estimated proceeds and what the proceeds will be used for
- Type and amount of securities offered, offering price, and selling and underwriting costs
- Stock options to be created in connection with the offering
- Copy of any prospectus, pamphlet, circular, or sales literature to be used in the offering
- Sample copy of the security along with opinion of counsel as to the legality of the security being offered
- Audited balance sheet current within four months of the offering with an income statement for three years before the balance sheet date

Effective Date

A Registration by Qualification becomes effective when the Administrator orders it effective

Notice Filing

The Administrator has the authority to require notice filings in the case of federal covered securities. Notice filing is primarily a way for the states to collect revenue from filing. In a notice filing the Administrator may require the following:

- Registration documents filed with the SEC
- Amendment documents filed with the initial registration statement
- A report of the value of the securities offered in the state
- Consent to service of process

Exemptions From Registration

The following securities are exempt from state registration:

- U.S. and Canadian government securities and municipal securities
- Foreign government securities
- Depository institutions
- Insurance company securities
- Public utility securities
- Federal covered securities
- Securities issued by nonprofit organizations
- Securities issued by cooperatives
- Securities of employee benefit plans
- Certain money market instruments

Exempt Transactions

- Isolated non-issuer transactions: secondary market transactions
- Unsolicited brokerage transactions: transactions initiated by the client
- Underwriter transactions: transactions between an issuer and an underwriter or between underwriters
- Bankruptcy, guardian, or conservator transactions:
- Institutional investor transactions: transactions primarily between financial institution
- Limited offering transactions: private placement offerings to no more than 10 persons other than institutional investors during the previous 12 consecutive months
- Pre-organization certificates: an offer or sale of a pre-organization certificate is exempt if no commission is paid, the number of subscribers does not exceed 10 and no payment is made by any subscriber
- Transactions with existing security holders – exempt as long as no commissions or other form of payments are made
- Specified non-issuer transactions
- Non-issuer transactions by pledges (someone who received the security as collateral for a loan)
- Unit secured transactions
- Control transactions
- Rescission offers

Books and Financial Records

Customer correspondence and e-mails must be kept on record for a minimum of 3 years Customer trade confirmations must be kept for 3 years Customer account statements must be kept for 6 years

Maintaining Registration

Reports to Customers
(only applies to investment advisers)

The State Administrator can require investment advisers to furnish certain information to customers. Prospective customers are given an "Investment Advisory Brochure" at least 48 hours prior to entering into any investment advisory contract. This brochure gives full disclosure to the customer

Electronic record-keeping

Electronic record-keeping methods follow the same retention standards as paper records Electronic storage is permitted on any digital storage media The storage media must be non-rewritable and non-erasable. A separate duplicate copy my be retained in another location

Financial Reports

Broker-dealers and investment advisers must file financial reports with the Administrator as required. If a broker-dealer is registered with the SEC under the Securities and Exchange Act of 1934; or if an investment adviser is registered under the Investment Adviser's Act of 1940; this requirement may be met by filing the Federally required reports with the State

Inaccurate Information

If any filing with the State Administrator is found to have material errors or omissions, the registrant must file a correcting amendment promptly. If the amendment corrects an initial registration application, the registration does not become effective until 30 days have elapsed from the filing of the amendment

Inspections

All records of registrants are subject to periodic examination by representatives of the Administrator. To avoid duplication of examinations, these reviews can be performed by representatives of FINRA or the SEC

Advertising and Sales Literature

These materials may be required to be filed with the State unless the security or transaction is exempt, or unless the security involved is a federal covered security. Included in the requirement are prospectuses, pamphlets, circulars, form letters, advertising and sales literature

Reasons registration can be denied, revoked, or suspended if:

- It is not in the best interest of the public
- The person who is in the subject of the order:
  - Has filed incomplete, false or misleading registration information
  - Has willfully violated the Act's provisions
  - Has been enjoined by court order from engaging in the securities business
  - Is subject of an order by the Administrator denying, suspending, or revoking registration as a broker-dealer, agent, investment adviser or investment adviser representative
  - Has been convicted of a misdemeanor involving any aspect of the securities business, or been convicted of any felony within the past 10 years
  - Is subject of a determination that the person has willfully violated the securities laws by an Administrator of another State or the SEC, within the past 10 years
  - Has engages in unethical or dishonest business practices
  - Is insolvent, which is defined as the inability to meet obligations as the come due
  - Is unqualified based on lack of experience, training and knowledge
  - Has failed to pay required fees to the State within 30 days after being notified by the Administrator
  - Has failed to properly supervise employees. This provision applies to broker-dealers and investment advisers. This does not apply to agents
  - Is no longer in existence; has ceased to do business as a broker-dealer, sales representative or investment adviser; cannot be located after a reasonable search; or has been adjudicated as mentally incompetent

Voluntary withdrawal from registration becomes effective 30 days after being filed by a broker-dealer
If there are legal proceedings against the person, withdrawal is not permitted

Definitions

Administrator: The office or agency responsible for administering the securities laws of the state. The Administrator has jurisdiction over all securities activity, and the registration of securities and securities professionals. The Administrator is also responsible for making rules and issuing orders.

The Administrator has to power to conduct investigations, publish information about violations, subpoena persons and records, compel testimony that incriminates, issue a cease and desist order without providing a hearing

Denial, Revocation or Suspension of Registration

The Administrator has the authority to issue a "stop order", denying effectiveness to registration

The Administrator can issue a stop order if:
- The registration statement is incomplete, misleading or false with respect to material facts
- The state securities laws have been willfully violated by any person involved in the offering
- The enterprise is illegal
- The security being registered is subject to an injunction (temporary or permanent) from another State or Federal court
- The issuer is using a registration method for which it is ineligible
- The offering is being made on terms that are unfair, unjust or inequitable
- The underwriter's compensation is unreasonable
- The offering tends to work a fraud on purchasers

Appealing Stop Orders

If a stop order is entered, the Administrator must notify all interested parties promptly with the reasons for the stop order issue, and that a hearing will be scheduled to take place within 15 days of a written request
The Administrator can issue a "cease and desist" order without providing a hearing

Liabilities and Penalties

Civil Liability
Civil liabilities are usually applied when a person violates the Act without intending to defraud or deceive. In this case, a customer that lost money must be paid back

If a person violates the Act in the process of selling securities, the person must buy back that security at the original price, pay interest on the monies invested at the legal rate in the State (6% in most State and pay the purchaser's legal fees

If the purchaser no longer owns the securities, the seller must pay the difference between the original price and the price at which the buyer sold the securities, plus interest and attorney's fees

Proceedings seeking criminal penalties have a 5-year statute of limitation – proceedings cannot start 5 years after the date of the alleged violation

Criminal Liability and Penalties
When a person violates the Act with the intention to defraud or deceives, or if that person commits a serious felony criminal liabilities and penalties apply. In this case the customer must be paid back with interest, the person who violated the Act may have to pay fines and/or face jail time

Offer of Rescission

If a seller discovers that he illegally offered a security to a purchaser, he may offer to repurchase the securities under the conditions discussed under the civil liabilities obligations. The offer to repurchase the securities must be made in writing and include:

- How the violation occurred
- Any information necessary to correct the error
- An offer to repurchase the securities for cash
- A statement stating the offer must be accepted within 30 days in writing

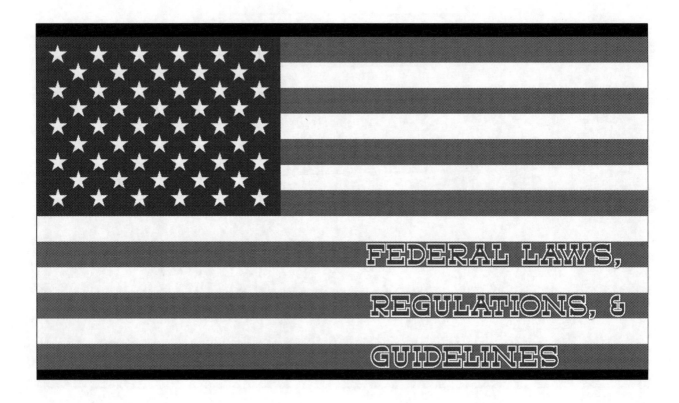

The Securities Act of 1933

The Securities Act of 1933 was created in response
to the stock market crash of 1929 to protect investors
against fraud concerning the issuance of securities. The
act requires securities issuers to make full disclosure
of all material information in their registration materials
(filed with the SEC) in order for investors to make fully
informed investing decisions

Definitions

Security: an instrument that constitutes an investment of money in a common enterprise with the expectation of profits primarily from the efforts of a person other than the investor. A common enterprise is an enterprise where the funds of an investor is interwoven with the funds of another investor or the enterprise offering the security

Equity Security: a stock (common or preferred), a security convertible into a common stock or right or warrant to purchase a stock

Municipal Securities: any security that is a direct obligation of, or guaranteed by, a state or any political subdivision thereof.

Government Securities: securities that are direct obligations of the U.S. Government. This also includes government agencies such as Fannie Mae)

Issuer:
Any person who issues, or proposes to issue, securities.

Prospectus
A summary of the registration statement. The prospectus contains all material information found in the registration statement in shorter form. The prospectus must be sent to every investor solicited and every investor who purchases a new security issue

Red Herring
A red herring is a preliminary prospectus. The red herring is sent to prospective purchasers to determine interest in the new issue. It is sent during the 20-day cooling off period – the period between filing the registration statement with the SEC and the effective date (when the security can begin trading). Broker/dealers may not accept orders under any circumstance during the cooling off period.

At the end of the 20-day cooling off period the issue becomes effective and can begin trading. If the registration statement is inadequate or missing material information, the SEC may issue a stop order, also known as a cease and desist order, to suspend the effective date

Exemptions

The following are exempt from registering under the Act:

Federal government and municipal issues
Commercial paper that mature in 9 months (270) from the date they are issued
Any security issued by a religious, educational, charitable, or not-for-profit institution
Any security issued by a federal or state bank
Any interest in a railroad equipment trust

The following are exempt under the Act of 1933 but not Uniform Act
Any security offered at an amount less than $5 million during a 12-month period (Regulation A)
Any security issued only to persons that reside in a single state or territory where the issuer is also a resident (Rule 147)
At least 80% of the issuer's gross revenue must be from one state
At least 80% of the proceeds from the offering must be used within the state
At least 80% of the issuer's assets must be located within the state Exemptions

The following securities are exempt under the Uniform Securities Act but not under the Securities Act of 1933:

- Foreign government securities
- Federal covered securities listed on a national exchange or Nasdaq
- Securities issued by insurance companies

Exempted transactions

Transactions by persons other than an issuer or underwriter
Private placement transactions

Liabilities Under the Act of 1933

Under the Act of 1933, individuals are subject to criminal prosecution if false and misleading statements were made intentionally in the registration statement or the prospectus.

The civil liabilities codes allow purchasers of a security whose registration statement contains false or misleading information of material fact to sue:

- Every person who signed the registration form
- All directors of the issuer
- Attorneys
- Accountants
- Appraisers or other experts
- Underwriters
- Parent companies

A person can be exempt from liability if that person can prove, after investigation, that he had reason to believe the statements in the registration statement are accurate

The statute of limitation for bringing actions against violations is the earlier of one year after the discovery of the violation or three years after the date of the action

Federal Covered Security

A federal covered security is defined as one that is:

Listed on the NYSE, American Stock Exchange, or NASDAQ, or is a senior security (preferred stock or bonds)
Issued by a registered investment company
Sold to qualified purchasers
Sold in exempt transactions specified by the Securities Act of 1933

Federal covered securities only have to register with the SEC and not a State

Investment Adviser Act of 1940

Federal legislation that defines "investment adviser" and requires investment advisers to register with the SEC or with the states in which they do business

The Investment Adviser Act of 1940 regulates persons in the business of giving investment advice and establishes standards of ethical business conduct

Definitions

Investment Adviser: Any person who offers investment advice, reports or analyses with respect to securities for compensation

The definition above includes financial planners, pension consultants, and sports entertainment representatives

The following are excluded from the definition of an investment adviser under federal law:

A bank or bank holding company
Lawyers, accountants, teachers or engineers
Broker/dealers whose performance of such services are incidental to their role as broker/dealers
Publishers of any bonafide newspaper, news magazine, or business or financial publication of general and regular circulation
Any person whose investment advice is solely in regards to securities issued or guaranteed by the government

These persons are also excluded in the definition under state law

Fiduciary: a person legally authorized to hold and manage assets in a trust for another person

The definitions of a person, a broker and a dealer are the same under the Investment Adviser Act of 1940 as they are under state and federal laws

Registration Requirements

The Investment Act of 1940 requires every person who engages in giving investment advice as a primary business to register with the SEC or a state

The following are exempt from registration requirements:

Advisers whose clients live in the state in which the adviser has its primary place of business and who do not give advice on securities listed on any national exchange
Advisers who only have insurance companies as clients
Advisers who have had fewer than 15 clients in the previous 12 months, none of which is an investment company registered with the SEC

Registration Procedures Under Federal Law

Form ADV: the standard registration form under the Investment Advisers Act. It is made up of two parts: schedule I and II. Schedule I is filed with the SEC and Schedule II is kept on file by the company and must be readily accessible at the adviser's principal office. Once the form is filed it remains in the adviser's permanent records

Schedule I: the adviser must prove it has at least $25 million under management on schedule I. Advisers are required to file Form ADV-schedule I no later than 90 days after the last day of their fiscal year

Updating: changes in name, business location, contact person preparing the form, organizational structure must updated promptly on Form ADV

Fees: an initial fee must be paid at registration and at annual renewals

Form ADV-W: this form is filed when a business wants to withdraw registration voluntarily. The form becomes effective 60 days after being filed with the SEC

Federal Covered Advisers

Federal Covered Advisers are defined as:

- Investment advisers that manage $25 million or more of assets
- Investment advisers to registered investment companies

- Federal covered advisers must registered with the SEC and are not required to register in their State
- Advisers with between $25 million and $30 million under management have the choice of registering with the SEC or their State, thus truly requiring SEC registration when an advisor is managing $30 million in assets

The following must register with the SEC:

- Nationally recognized statistical ratings organizations (Moody's or Standard & Poor's)
- Newly formed advisers that reasonably expect to have at least $25 million of assets under management within 120 days of formation
- A State registered adviser that is an affiliate of an SEC registered adviser
- An adviser that is required to be registered in 30 or more states

Books and Records Required by The Investment Adviser Act of 1940

The SEC and the states require the following:

- A journal containing cash receipts and disbursement records
- General auxiliary ledgers reflecting asset, liability, reserve, capital, income and expense accounts
- A memorandum of each order given by the adviser, or any instruction received by the adviser from the client, and any modification to orders
- All checkbooks, bank statements, canceled checks, and cash reconciliations
- All bills or statements paid or unpaid
- all trial balances, financial statements and internal audit working papers
- Originals of all written communications received by the adviser and copies of all communications sent out to the customer regarding securities transactions
- A record of all accounts in which the advisor has any discretionary authority
- Copies or originals of powers of attorney granting discretionary authority
- All written agreements regarding the advisor's business
- A record of all securities transactions in which the adviser has a beneficial ownership
- A file containing all advertisements and sales literature, including electronic media, circulated by the adviser. If a specific recommendation was made concerning a security without stating the reasons for that recommendation, a special memorandum must be prepared indicating the reasons for that recommendation

Investment Adviser Representative

Investment Adviser Representatives are defined as:

- Any partner, officer, director, or other individual employed by an investment adviser who:
- Makes recommendations or renders advice regarding securities
- Manages accounts or portfolios of clients
- Determines which recommendations or advice regarding securities should be given
- Solicits, offers, or negotiates for the sale of investment advisory services
- Supervises employees who perform any of the functions listed above

Employees who solely perform clerical or ministerial duties are excluded from the definition of an investment adviser

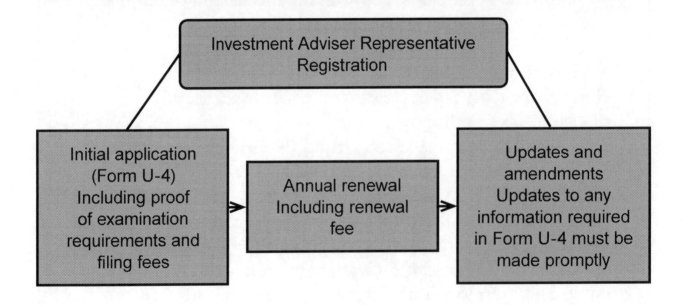

Investment Adviser Representative Registration

Initial application (Form U-4) Including proof of examination requirements and filing fees

Annual renewal Including renewal fee

Updates and amendments Updates to any information required in Form U-4 must be made promptly

Ethical Practices and Fiduciary Obligations

Misrepresentations

Registered representatives may not misrepresent themselves or their services to their clients. This definition includes qualifications, experience, education, nature of services offered, and fees to be charged

Selling Away

Private securities transactions-buying or selling securities outside of a representative's regular business and his employing member firm—is known as selling away. A representative must notify his employer of the proposed transaction in writing, describing the proposed transaction in detail, his role, and whether he has or will receive compensation for the transaction. If the representative has or will receive compensation, his employer may approve or disapprove of the transaction

Investment Discretion

When a person has the authority to determine which securities will be purchased or sold and the amount to be purchased or sold, that person exercises investment discretion

Investment Recommendations

Investment recommendations must be in the best interest of the client and not the representative's. A representative must fully explain the risks involved in any recommended investment. Investment recommendations must be consistent with the customer's needs, financial capability, objectives, and risk tolerance

Guaranteeing and Sharing in profits and losses

A representatives may not guarantee profits on an investment. Representatives are also prohibited from sharing in profits and losses in a client's account. An exception is if a joint account has received the member firm's prior approval and sharing of profits and losses are proportionate to the representative's contributions to the account

Borrowing and Lending

Firms that allow lending and borrowing between representatives and customers must have written procedures to monitor those activities. Registered representatives must provide written notification and get approval from their member firm. The following arrangements are permitted:

- There is an immediate family relationship between the representative and the customer
- The customer is in the business of lending money
- The customer and the representative are registered with the same firm
- The customer and the representative have a personal or business relationship outside the broker-customer relationship

The Securities and Exchange Act of 1934

While the Securities Act of 1933 regulates new issues (the primary market) the Securities and Exchange Act of 1934 regulates the secondary market. The Act also created the Securities and Exchange Commission (SEC) which holds disciplinary powers over regulated entities and all persons associated with them

The SEC

The SEC enforces all federal laws regulating the securities industry, except those regulating credit. There are five people that make up the SEC; one serving as chair. All five people are appointed by the U.S. president with the advice and consent of the Senate. Each commissioner serves a 5-year terms. The terms are staggered so that a new commissioner is appointed each year. Commissioners may not have any other business or employment during their term. They are also prohibited from engaging in any securities transactions other than US government securities. All securities owned before being appointed are placed into a blind trust

Powers of the SEC

The SEC has the authority to investigate violations of the federal securities laws. The SEC can also investigate the violations of the rules of the SROs

Although SROs have their own procedures for enforcing their own rules, that does not limit the SEC's authority to investigate and/or obtain court injunction

The SEC has the power to:
- **Administer oaths**
- **Subpoena witnesses**
- **Compel attendance**
- **Require books and records to be produced**
- **Suspend trading in any nonexempt security for up to 10 days with prior notice**
- **Suspend trading on an entire exchange for of up to 90 days**

SEC Rule 15c3-1 (Uniform Net Capital Rule)

The Uniform Net Capital Rule establishes minimum net capital rules for broker/dealers. A firm must always have a minimum amount of net capital to protect its customers. The broker/dealer will not be allowed to operate if it does not meet the minimum requirement

The SEC is the appropriate regulatory agency for the following:

- **National securities exchanges**
- **Registered securities associations**
- **Members of an exchange or association**
- **Persons associated with a member**
- **Applicants to become a member or person associated with a member**
- **Municipal Securities Rulemaking Board**

The SEC does NOT regulate banks and other similar financial institutions

---

Investment Discretion

When a person has the authority to determine which securities will be purchased or sold and the amount to be purchased or sold, that person exercises investment discretion

Statutory Disqualification: a person may be subject to statutory disqualification from an SRO if that person:

- has been suspended or expelled from any SRO, commodities market or futures trading association

- is subject to a suspension or registration revocation for a period of 12 months or less

- is the cause of a broker-dealer suspension because of conduct while associated with a broker or dealer

- has been convicted of a securities violation or misdemeanor within the past 10 years

- is subject to an injunction (permanent or temporary) from a competent court jurisdiction prohibiting that person from engaging in the securities business

- has willfully violated securities laws

Registration under the Securities Exchange Act of 1934

Groups and organizations required to register with the SEC:

- Brokers and dealers operating in interstate commerce, on exchanges and over-the-counter
- Securities exchanges
- National securities associations (MSRB, NASD)
- Corporations with listed securities

- Corporate applications to the SEC must include:
  - The organization, its structure and nature of the business
  - The terms, position, rights, and privileges of the different classes of outstanding securities
  - The directors, officers and underwriting and each person holding 10% or more of the corporation's securities
  - Certified balance sheets for the previous three fiscal years
  - Certified profit and loss statements for the previous three fiscal years

Exemptions

The following are exempt from registering und the Act:

Federal government and municipal issues
Commercial paper that mature in 9 months (270) from the date
they are issued
Any security issued by a religious, educational, charitable, or
not-for-profit institution
Any security issued by a federal or state bank
Any interest in a railroad equipment trust

The following are exempt under the Act of 1933
but not Uniform Act
Any security offered at an amount less than $5 million during a
12-month period (Regulation A)
Any security issued only to persons that reside in a single state
or territory where the issuer is also a resident **(Rule 147)**
At least 80% of the issuer's gross revenue must be from one
state
At least 80% of the proceeds from the offering must be used
within the state
At least 80% of the issuer's assets must be located
within the state

Definitions

Self-Regulatory Organization (SRO): a non-governmental organization that has the power to create and enforce industry regulations and standards, such as FINRA

Exchange: A marketplace in which securities, commodities, derivatives and other financial instruments are traded

Equity Security: a stock (common or preferred), a security convertible into a common stock or right or warrant to purchase a stock

Municipal Securities: any security that is a direct obligation of, or guaranteed by, a state or any political subdivision thereof.

Government Securities: securities that are direct obligations of the U.S. Government. This also includes government agencies such as Fannie Mae)

Restricted Securities: Restricted securities are securities purchased by a control person in a private placement offering. Investors must sign an investment letter stating that they understand the restrictions involved in reselling the security

Control person: a director, officer, the owner of 10% of more of voting stocks and the spouse of any of the preceding control person. Control persons are also referred to as insiders or affiliates

Control stock: a control stock is stock owned by a control person

Nonaffiliate: any investor who is not a control person and has no other affiliation with the issuer other than being a stockholder

The following securities are exempt under the Uniform Securities Act but not under the Securities Act of 1933:

- Foreign government securities
- Federal covered securities listed on a national exchange or Nasdaq
- Securities issued by insurance companies

Exempted transactions

Transactions by persons other than an issuer or underwriter
Private placement transactions

SEC Regulation D

SEC rule 506 which provides an exemption for security offers and sales made to less than 35 unaccredited investors (the amount of accredited investors allowed to keep exempt status is unlimited). Unsophisticated investors must be represented by a representative (lawyer, accountant or financial advisor to take part in the offering. General advertising and solicitation are prohibited under Regulation D offerings.

Regulation D is aimed at facilitating the securities offering process for small businesses

SEC Rule 501 defines accredited investors as:

- Institutional investors,
- Directors, executive officers and general partners of the issuer,
- Any natural person with a net worth, or joint net worth with a spouse, of $1 million,
- Individuals with yearly income of at least $200,000 in each of the past two years and can reasonably expect to have income of $200,000 in the current year – the income requirement is $300,000 when combined with a spouse's income,
- Entities made up accredited investors

Rule 503 (Form D)

Form D must be filed no later than 15 days after the first sale of securities in the offering by an issuer that issuing securities under Regulation D

Form D includes information such as the total size of the offering, the amount sold to date, how proceeds will be used, and the names of any persons paid commissions

Securities issued under Regulation D are classified as "federal covered" securities and are exempt from state registration and qualification requirements

SEC Rule 144

Rule 144 was created to facilitate the resale of already existing restricted securities. The sale of an already existing restricted security does not require the filing of a complete registration statement with the SEC

Filings

Schedule D: requires a beneficial owner of 5% or more of securities registered under Securities Exchange Act of 1934 to file a report with the issuer, the SEC and the exchange on which the securities are listed within 10 days of any transactions. The filing must include the name and background of the person acquiring the securities, the origination of the money for the acquisition and the purpose of acquiring the securities

Section 13(f): requires institutional investment managers that exercise investment discretion over an equity portfolio with a market value of $100 million or more to file a Form 13F with the SEC every quarter within 45 days of the end of the quarter.

Schedule G: created for passive owners of 5% or more of a registered security. Those investors can file a Schedule G instead of a Schedule D. A passive investor is an investor who can certify that they did not purchase the securities for the purpose of changing or influence control over the issuer and hold no more than 20% of the issuer's securities

Section 16: requires insiders to file transaction reports before the end of the second business day following the day on which they executed a transaction

Margin Requirements

Regulation T

Regulation T delegates the board of governors of the Federal Reserve Boards to set margin requirements. The margin requirements determine how much money broker/dealers may lend their customers when purchasing securities on margin.

The Regulation T requirement is now set at 50%-a customer must deposit 50% of the value of the cost of securities purchased on margin.

New issues may not be bought on margin for 30 days after they are issued. Mutual funds cannot be bought on margin. Both new issues and mutual funds can be used as collateral for a loan after being held for 35 days.

The use of the following manipulative, deceptive and fraudulent practices are outlawed by the Act of 1934:

Churning: excessive trading by a broker/dealer in a discretionary account to generate commissions

Wash sale: the simultaneous sale and purchase of a security through the same broker/dealer. This is done to create an appearance of activity in a security. This is not related to a wash sale for tax purpose, when a security is bought and sold less than 30 days later

Matched orders: simultaneous sale and purchase of a security at the same price through different broker/dealers

Pegging, fixing and stabilizing: attempts to create a price level that would be otherwise be the result of the forces of supply and demand (stabilizing is allowed in certain cases in new issues)

Order tickets

- Order tickets are required before an order entry. The following have to be disclosed:
- Account number
- Whether the order was solicited, unsolicited or discretionary
- If a sale was long or short
- Aggregate value of bonds
- Time stamp showing the time the order was entered

Insider Transactions

- Officers or directors, and persons owning 10% or more of the securities of an issuer are defined as insiders
- The SEC must be notified of any changes in the ownership of securities owned by insiders
- Insiders are prohibited from short selling and from buying and selling those securities within a 6-month period (short-swing profits)

An insider is in violation of ITSFEA when he trades securities on non-public material information or when he passes on this information to another person who uses that information. Persons that are not insiders are also subject to the rules governing the use of non-public information.

This act gives the SEC the authority to pursue civil penalties against persons violating the provisions of this act. Civil penalties can be the greater of $1 million or three times any gains or losses avoided as a result of insider information. The penalty is used to pay bounties to informants. Criminal penalties could include jail time of up to 20 years.

The statute of limitation under this law is 5 years. No action may be brought under this section more than 5 years after the date of the last transaction that is the subject of the violation

Penalties for violating the law may not exceed to profit made or lost avoided

Securities Amendments Act of 1975

Signed into law by President Ford on June 4, 1975, this act amended some parts of the Acts of 1933 and 1934. Its main purpose was to remove any barriers to competition in the securities industry.

Fixed commissions were abolished and replaced with negotiated commissions on public orders
The SEC was directed to develop a national market system
The SEC was given the power to approved or refuse to approve any rules proposed by the exchanges, FINRA or the MSRB
Municipal securities dealers are required to register with the SEC
The SEC was given the power to regulate the activities of clearing corporations, securities depositories and transfer agents

Investment Company Act of 1940

An investment company is defined as any issuer that is or holds itself out as being engaged primarily in the business of investing, reinvesting, or trading in securities. More than 40% of the value of the issuer's total assets must be invested in investment securities for the issuer to be considered an investment company

Not included in this definition are:

- Broker/dealers
- Banks and savings and loans
- Insurance companies
- Holding companies
- Issuers whose securities are beneficially owned by no more than 100 persons
- Issuers who trade in investments other than securities

Types of Investment Companies

Face-amount certificate company

An investment company that issues face-amount certificates on the installment plan. A face-amount certificate represents an obligation by its issuer to pay a fixed sum on a stated date to certificate holders. These certificates are backed by security interest on assets such as real property or other securities.

Unit investment trust (UIT)

An investment company without a board of directors and only issues redeemable securities. UITs are not actively managed and have a fixed portfolio

Management company

An investment company other than a face-amount certificate company or a UIT. These companies typically have an investment manager who receives a fee based on assets under management

Management Companies

Open end: the term "open end" is synonymous with "mutual fund". Open-end shares are issued continually. Purchases of open-end shares are always done at net asset value (NAV) plus a sales charge. NAV is calculated at the end of every trading day. Shares are also redeemed at NAV

Closed-end: generally have a onetime issue and do not redeem shares. Shares are traded in the secondary market (like stocks). Share prices are based on supply and demand. Shares may be sold at, below (discount), or above (premium) NAV

Diversified: to be a diversified company, a management company must have at 75% of its assets invested with no more than 5% of total assets in one security. A diversified investment company can hold no more than 10% of the outstanding voting shares of any issue

Nondiversified: any management company other than a diversified management company

Registration of Investment Companies

Investment companies must registered with the SEC. In the registration the company must describe investment objectives, sales loads, whether they will be concentrating investments in a particular industry or group of industries

Ineligibility

Certain persons are prohibited from serving as advisers, principal underwriters, director member of an advisory board, officer of investment companies. These persons include:

- Anyone who has been convicted of any felony or misdemeanor involving the sale or purchase of any security
- Anyone temporarily or permanently enjoined by order, judgment, or decree of any court of competent jurisdiction from acting in any phase of the securities business
-

Those persons may file with the SEC to become eligible again

12-b-1 Rule

This rule allows open-end investment companies to issue their own shares without an underwriter and to charge an asset-based sales load. No load funds are permitted to charge a sales load as long as the load is used in activities in connection with the distribution of shares (pay commission to broker/dealers who sell shares of the fund). A fund may not used the term "no-load" if its 12b-1 fees exceed .25%

A mutual fund may act as a distributor of its own shares as long as asset-based sales loads are paid according to a written plan agreed upon by a majority of shareholders and is approved initially and re-approved annually by the Board of Directors

Investment companies may not:
Purchase on margin
Have a joint account with another person
Sell securities short
Own more than 3% of another investment company

Policy Changes

A majority vote of the outstanding stock is required to make investment policy changes such as changing from closed-end to open-end, from diversified to non-diversified, change in investment objective

Investment Company Size

Registered Investment Companies are required to have a net worth of at least $100,000 in order to be able to make a public offering

Investment Adviser Contracts

Investment advisers and principal underwriters of investment companies must have a contract approved by a majority vote of shareholders describing all compensation paid. If the contract is renewed after the first two years, the contract must be renewed annually by a majority of shareholders or the Board of Directors

Transactions of Certain Affiliated Persons and Underwriters

- Affiliated persons (persons who own 5% or more of the outstanding shares) may not knowingly sell any security to an investment company unless it was issued by that company itself
- Affiliated persons may not borrow money from the fund
- Affiliated persons may not buy any securities from that company besides the company's shares

Sales Charge

Redeemable securities can be sold with a reduced sales charge or no sales charge in certain circumstances:

- **A sales charge may be reduced with the use of a breakpoint**
  - **A breakpoint is a quantity level (number of shares purchased) at which investors receive a reduced sales charge**
  - **Persons that are excluded from taking advantages include investment clubs, purchases by an entity with no purpose other than making this investment**

- **There is no sales charge in sales to employees of the fund, the adviser or principal underwriter and shares purchased through automatic reinvestment of dividend and capital gains**

Reporting

Investment companies must send their financial reports and customer statements to customers at least semiannually

Money Laundering

Disguising financial assets and using them in such a way that they can be utilized without detecting the illegal activity that produced them is money laundering

Currency Transaction Reports (CTRs)

According to the Bank Secrecy Act financial institutions are required to file a CTR on FinCen Form 104 for every cash transaction that exceeds $10,000 and wire transfers of $3000. This applies to cash transactions to pay off loans, electronic transfers, or the purchase of securities and other investments

A series of small deposits totaling $10,000 made over a short period of time (structured transactions) are also included in this requirement. Numerous accounts with a firm must also be monitored closely

Common Stock is considered an EQUITY Security and represents ownership in a corporation.

<u>Investors who buy stocks:</u>
- Buy an ownership stake in a company's net worth
- Are entitled to a share in the company's profits
- Have equal votes on directors and other important matters

Note: Stockholders are not involved in their company's day-to-day operations

Benefits and risks of owning stocks:

Benefits:

Risks:

Benefits:
- Capital gains (Growth)

- Income (Dividends)

- Voting rights – the right to vote for corporate directors and other important matters

- Transferability – the ability to sell or give shares away
- Limited Liability – investors can only lose the capital invested

Risks:
- Price of stock decreases (market risk)

- Change in dividend policy – the board of directors my elect to keep a higher portion of earnings for things such as an acquisition or other business operations

- Low priority at bankruptcy – stockholders are last line to receive money from liquidated assets
- Business risk – the risk that the business may not perform as expected

Preferred stocks

Preferred stocks are equity securities and also share characteristics of fixed income securities

Because of their similarity to fixed income securities, preferred stocks' prices tend to fluctuate with changes in interest rates instead of the company's business prospects, unless there are dramatic changes in the company's ability to pay dividends

Benefits:

Dividends – owners of preferred stocks are paid before common stock owners when dividends are declared

Fixed Dividends

Risks:

Preferred stock owners are paid only before common stock owners at liquidation

No maturity – although preferred stocks share characteristics of debt securities, unlike debt, preferred stocks do not have a maturity date

Real Estate Investment Trust (REIT)

Retirement Plans: 1.2

A REIT is a company that manages a portfolio investments to earn profits for shareholders. Similar to investment company, REITs pool investors' capital and investors receive dividends from income and capital gains distributions. REITs give investors the opportunity to invest in real estate without the liquidity risks of direct property ownership

The following are characteristics of REITS:

- Trades on Stock Exchange and OTC
- Issues shares of beneficial interest representing an undivided interest in a pool of real estate investment
- Shares are not redeemable
- Have a negative correlation with the stock market
- Dividends are taxed at ordinary income

Fixed Income Securities (Debt)

Fixed income securities represent money loaned to a corporation, the U.S governments, States, Municipalities, and U.S. Territories by investors. In return for the loan, investors receive interest payments regularly over a period of time until the security matures, at which point investors receive full principle payment. Debt financing is typically long term-longer than 5 years.

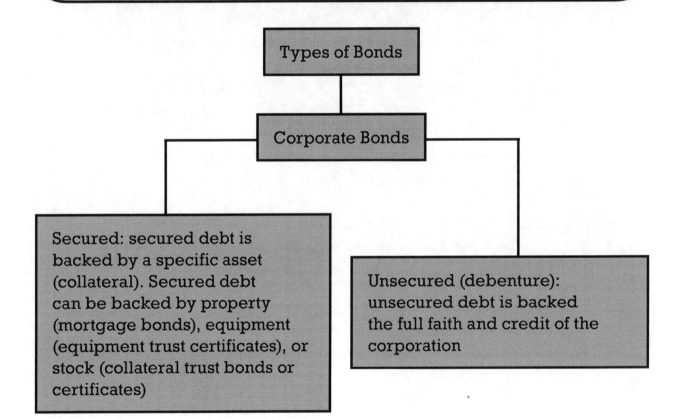

Types of Bonds

Corporate Bonds

Secured: secured debt is backed by a specific asset (collateral). Secured debt can be backed by property (mortgage bonds), equipment (equipment trust certificates), or stock (collateral trust bonds or certificates)

Unsecured (debenture): unsecured debt is backed the full faith and credit of the corporation

Types of Bonds

Municipal Bonds

General Obligation (GO): GO bonds are backed by the full faith, credit and taxing power of the municipality by which it is issued. Ad valorem taxes (property taxes) are primarily used to pay debt service on GO bonds

Revenue Bonds: Revenue bonds are issued to finance a revenue-producing enterprise such as a toll bridge, a water or electric system, an airport, etc. Revenues from that enterprise is used to pay the bonds' debt service

US Government Bonds

T-Bills: short-tem obligations of the US government. They are issued every week through a competitive bidding process. T-bills have maturities of 4 weeks, 13 weeks, 26 weeks, and 52 weeks. T-bills are issued at a discount, mature at par and do not pay interest. The difference between the discount and par value is received at maturity and is considered interest income

T-Notes: medium-term obligations of the US Treasury. T-Notes pay semi-annual interest, have maturities of 2-10 years, and mature at par

T-Bonds: like T-Notes, T-bonds are direct, long term obligations of the US Treasury. T-bonds pay semi-annual interest, have maturities of 10-20 years, and mature at par

Treasury Inflation Protection Securities (TIPS): TIPS are a special type of Treasury issue that protects investors against purchasing power risk. The are issued with a fixed interest rate but the amount is adjusted semi-annually according to the change in the Consumer Price Index (CPI)

Government Agency Bonds

Federal National Mortgage Association (FNMA): Fannie Mae is a former government-owned agency that was converted to a private corporation. Fannie Mae primarily purchases mortgages that are insured by the Federal Housing Administration or guaranteed by the Veterans Administration, and issues mortgage-backed bonds to investors. Fannie Mae bonds are issued at par, and pay semi-annual interest

Government National Mortgage Association (GNMA): Ginnie Mae issues pass-through certificates that represent an interest in pools of FHA-insured, or VA or Farmers Home Administration-guaranteed mortgages. Monthly mortgage payments are collected in the pool and the shares "pass through" to investors.

Investment Company Securities

Benefits of owning investment company securities:

- Diversification/safety
- Professional management
- Liquidity
- Minimum initial investment

Risks:

- Equity funds are subject to market risk and bond funds are subject to interest rate risk
- Fees and expenses – sales charges, 12b-1 fees and possibly redemption fees
- A mutual fund may allow a breakpoint, which helps investors reduce sales charges

Alternative Investments

Hedge Funds

A hedge fund is a type of fund that does not have to register with the SEC, unlike other investment companies. Hedge funds are allowed to engage in risky investment strategies such as arbitrage, shorting stocks in bearish markets, and using leverage and derivatives.

Management fees also tend to be much higher in hedge funds than other investment companies. Almost all hedge funds charge performance-based fees. Because of the level of risk taken by hedge funds, they are limited to institutional clients and accredited investors. Ordinary investors can invest in hedge funds indirectly through funds of hedge funds.

Limited Partnerships

Limited partnerships, also known as Direct Participation Programs (DPP), allow the economic consequences of a business to flow through to investors. DPPs do not pay dividends, instead they pass income, gains, losses, deductions, and credits directly to investors. DPP gains are only taxed when received by investor, therefore double taxation is avoided in DPP investments. Limited partners have limited liability, meaning they cannot lose more than they have invested.

The greatest disadvantage of investing in a DPP is liquidity risk. It is very difficult for investors to locate potential buyers. Passive losses from DPPs may only be deducted against passive income for tax purposes

Variable Annuities

A life insurance company product designed to provide supplemental income. Investors pay a premiums that are invested in a general account. A company is obligated to pay a guaranteed a specified amount based on how much was paid in

Types of Annuities

Fixed
Fixed monthly payments
Subject to purchasing power risk
Insurance company assumes risks

Variable
Variable monthly payments (keeps pace with inflation)
Protects against purchasing power
Investor assumes risks
Variable annuities are securities

Annuities payments can also be made in lump sums

Contributions are made with after-tax dollars unless annuities are held in an employee sponsored retirement plan or IRA

Contributions with after-tax dollars are not taxed at withdrawal

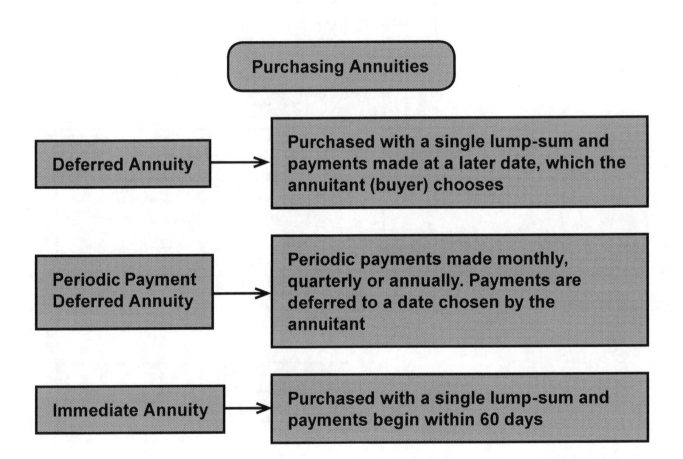

Accumulation Stage

The accumulation stage is the pay-in period (when an annuitant makes payments towards an annuity). The contract between the annuitant and the company is flexible. The annuitant can miss periodic payments without penalty. The annuitant can also terminate the contract at any time during the accumulation stage, however surrender charges may be paid on withdrawals within the first five to 10 years.

Accumulation units: an accounting measure that represents the shares an investor owns in the separate account. The value in the unit changes with the value of the securities in the separate account.

ANNUITIZATION PHASE (PAYOUT PHASE)

Usually begins at 59 ½ because any prior distribution is subject to 10% penalty

LIFE ONLY
Investors will be paid a certain amount for as long as they live.

LIFE WITH PERIOD CERTAIN (ex: 10years)
- **The annuities will be paid for as long as they live.**
- **If not for 10 years, then a beneficiary will be paid up to the 10th year.**

LIFE WITH FULL SURVIVOR
- **The annuitant will be paid for as long as they live.**
- **When they die, the beneficiary gets the remainder for as long as they live**

- **The difference between fixed and variable is once the payment is set on a fixed annuity, the value does not change.**
- **The variable annuity payments will increase or decrease based on the return of the fund.**

At payout, accumulation units become annuity unit. Annuity units are an accounting measures that determines the amount of each payment during the payment period

Taxation of Annuities

The total amount of contributions made with after-tax dollars in annuities are not taxed at withdrawal. Any money in excess of contributions (capital gains, interest, dividends) is taxed as ordinary income

Random withdrawals are taxed under "last in, first out" (LIFO) method. Those withdrawal are taxed as ordinary income until all earnings above contributions are withdrawn. At which point withdrawals are not taxed.

Lump sump withdrawals are taxed in a similar fashion as random withdrawals. Withdrawals of earnings before age 59½ are taxed as ordinary income and are subject to an additional 10% penalty.

Benefits of investing in annuities:

- Tax-deferred growth
- Guaranteed death benefit: if the investor dies during the accumulation period, a beneficiary will receive the greater of the amount invested or the current value of the account
- Guaranteed lifetime income
- IRS Section 1035 transfers: accounts can be transferred without tax consequences
- No age 70½ requirements
- No probate: the account passes directly without the time and expense of probate upon death

Life Insurance

A life insurance policy is a contract between an insurance company and an individual designed to provide financial compensation to a named beneficiary in the case of the individual's death

Term Insurance → Term insurance is the least expensive form of life insurance. They provide protection for a specified period of time (one year, five years, 10 years, 30 years or to a specified age). If the insured purchases a term life insurance for a 10-year term at 65 and dies at 66, the insured receives no money

Whole Life Insurance (WLI) → Unlike term insurance, WLI provides protection for as long as the insured lives. The benefit payable and the premium is set at the time of the of policy's issue and remains that way throughout the policy's life

Cash values
Whole life insurance combines a death benefit with an accumulation element. The accumulation is the policy's cash value and increases each year the policy is kept

Policy Loans
An insured person's cash value cannot be forfeited. Once cash value is accumulated the insured can cash in a policy at any time or borrow a portion of the cash value (policy loan). Policy loans decrease the face value of the policy if the insured dies before the loan is repaid

Universal Life Insurance

→

Universal life insurance was created in response to the low interest rates earned by WLIs in periods of high inflation. Universal life insurance policies can earn interests of up to 12%. Unlike whole life, universal life policies allows an insurer to adjust the death benefits and premiums. Universal life contracts are subject to two insurance rates: the current annual rate, which coincides with current market conditions, and the contract rate, which is the minimum guaranteed interest rate of the policy

Death benefits

Option 1:
The death benefit is equal to the face amount of the contract. As cash value increases, net death protection decreases over the life of the policy

Option 2:
Death benefits increases at an amount equal to the face value plus the cash account.

Policy loans
Universal life provides policy loans in the same manner as whole life policies. Universal life policies also allows cash withdrawals, also called a partial surrender. A partial surrender is not subject to interest rates and decreases the cash value of the account and has no effect on the face amount. If the partial surrender is paid back, it is treated as a premium payment

Variable Life Insurance

Premiums for variable life insurance is not invested in a general account as in whole life or universal insurance. Rather it is invested in a separate account and allows the insured has some choice as to what the premiums are invested in. Cash value in the fund fluctuates with the performance of the separate account and is not guaranteed. Variable life insurance policies have a minimum guaranteed death benefit, which may increase above the minimum depending on investment results in the account

Scheduled (Fixed) Premium Variable Life
Issued with a minimum guaranteed death benefit, a fixed VLI's premium is determined at issue and requires evidence of insurability. The premium is calculated according to the insured's age and sex, and the policy's face amount at issue

Flexible Premium Variable Life (Universal)
Flexible premium VLI allows flexible premiums and flexible death benefits. The insured has the option of increasing or reduce premium payments and must maintain a minimum cash value.

Deductions from the Separate Account
Deductions from the separate account reduces the investment return payable to the policy owner. Deductions from the separate account include mortality risk, expense risk fee, investment management

Deductions from the Premium
Deductions from the gross premium typically reduces the amount of money invested in the separate account. Charges deducted from premiums are administration fees (usually a one time fee), sales load-which much average out to 9% over a 20-year period, and state premium taxes

Contract Exchange
VLIs have the option of being switched to a traditional fixed-benefit WLI contract. The time period during which this switch is allowed varies from company to company but may not be, under federal law, less than 24 months

Voting Rights
Contract holders receive one vote per $100 of cash value funded by the separate account. Changes in investment objectives and other important matters require majority vote of the separate account's outstanding shares or by order of the state insurance commissioner

Taxing Life Insurance

Income Tax
Premiums are generally non-deductible and proceeds made to a beneficiary are generally exempt from federal income tax

Estate Tax
If the insured retains the right to name a beneficiary, choose how dividends or policy proceeds will be paid out, transfer ownership of an insurance policy, borrow money from the cash value of the policy, or perform any other functions that are rights of ownership, then that person has incidents of ownership. By having incidents of ownership in that policy, the entire death benefit payable is included for federal estate tax purposes in the insured individual's estate

Irrevocable Life Insurance Trust
Instead of owning a policy on one's own life, an individual may have the life insurance transferred to or acquired by an irrevocable life insurance trust (ILIT). By doing this, premiums paid by the insured may qualify for the annual gift tax exclusion of $13,000 per year per beneficiary

Derivatives

Options

An option gives the holder (buyer) the right, but not obligation to buy or sell an underlying instrument at a specific price

An option seller (writer) has the obligation to buy or sell an underlying instrument if it is exercised by the holder.

Types of Options
Call option—The right to buy the underlying instrument at a specific price
Put option—The right to sell the underlying instrument at a specific price

The "underlying instrument" can be anything with a fluctuating value

Each options contract represents 100 shares of the underlying instrument

Party #1
Buyer of Contract
Pays a Premium
Holder/Owner
Has RIGHTS

Party #2
Seller of Contract
Receives a Premium
Has OBLIGATIONS

Four Basic Option Fundamentals

Puts and Calls

Buy a Call (Bullish): give the investor a chance to speculate on the price of the stock increasing by making a relatively small investment. The most an investor can lose by buying a call is the premium paid

Sell a Call (Bearish): allows an investor to generate income, and hedge a long stock position. A call writer (seller) is obligated to sell a stock at a specified price if the option is exercised

Buy a Put (Bearish): allows an investor to speculate on the price of the stock decreasing. By buying a put the investor buys the right to sell a stock at a specific price. If the price of the stock falls, the investor can buy the stock at the low market price and exercise the put at the (higher) exercise price

Sell a Put (Bullish): allows an investor to generate income on speculation that the stock price will increase. If the stock price decreases and the option is exercised, the put writer has the obligation to buy the stock at the exercise price

Hedging With Options

Long stock and long puts: long puts protects an investor who a holds a long position in a stock. If the price of the stock declines, the investor can exercise the puts, which allows the investor to sell the stock at a price higher than the current market price

Long stock short calls (covered call writing): writing a covered call is when an investor sells a call when he also owns the underlying stock. The call writer generates income from the premium received from selling the call. If the call is exercised, the call writer must sell the stock at the exercise price. This causes the call writer to limit gain on the long position

Short stock and long calls: short selling is borrowing stocks, selling them, and buying the stock back when the price declines and returning the stock to the lender. The difference in price is the profit kept by an investor. The investor can hedge a short position by buying a call.

Short stock and short puts (covered put writing): a short position can also be protected by selling calls. However, at a certain point, the potential loss can be unlimited

Non-security Derivatives

Forward Contracts: Forward contracts are direct commitments between a buyer and a seller to buy and sell commodities. The seller is obligated to make delivery and the buyer is obligated to take delivery. The terms of the contract are defined by the buyer and seller without third party intervention. A forward contract typically consists of quantity of the commodity, quality of the commodity, time of delivery, place for delivery, and price to be paid at delivery

Futures: futures contracts are exchange traded obligations. Buyers are obligated to accept delivery and sellers are obligated to deliver. Futures contracts prices are computed daily and all accounts must be settled before the opening of trading on the next trading day

Secondary Market
(All stocks trade in secondary market (not open end mutual funds))

- Exchange market (first market)
  - Composed of NYSE and other exchanges
  - Maintain central marketplaces and trading floors
  - Double-auction system is used to execute trades at favorable prices
  - Specialists maintain a fair and orderly market in specific stocks they are responsible for by placing orders for their own accounts to either stabilize or facilitate trading when imbalance in supply and demand occur

- Over-the-counter (second market)
  - Inter-dealer market in which unlisted securities are traded
    - Thousands of securities and all municipal and government securities
  - Securities dealers are connected through computer and telephone across the country
  - OTC is divided into Nasdaq and non-Nasdaq
    - Nasdaq: Global Select Market, Global Market and Capital Market
    - Non-Nasdaq: consists of stocks in the Pink Sheets and on the OTC Bulletin
  - OTC system uses market makers – broker/dealers who stand ready to buy and sell in each stock they have published bid and ask quotes
  - When market makers raise their bid price the stock's market price increases; when they lower their ask price, the stock's market price decreases

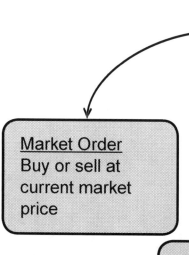

Types of Orders

Market Order
Buy or sell at current market price

Limit Orders
Limit the amount paid when buying securities or received when selling securities

Buy limit: order to buy at a price lower than current market price

Sell limit: order to sell at a price higher than the current market price

A customer risks missing an opportunity to buy or sell by placing a limit order

Stop Orders
Designed to protect a profit or prevent loss if stock moves in the wrong direction

Buy stop: Protects profits or limits loss on short position—placed above market price

Sell stop: Protects profits or limits loss on a long position – placed below market price

Stop limit: Order that, once triggered, becomes a limit order
• Become a market order once the stock trades at or moves through stop price
• A trade at the stop price triggers the order

Individual Account

An individual account may be for a person, a trust or a deceased person through an estate account. Individual accounts are typically managed by an adviser for a fee. Advisers must establish an Investment Policy Statement, which includes of investment objectives and strategy, before executing trades on a client's behalf. Advisers must also review the client's investment profile periodically in order to make changes in objectives and strategy if necessary

Joint Accounts

Joint with rights of survivorship (JTWROS)
- If one of the parties dies then the account is automatically transferred into the name of the survivor.

Tenants in Common (JIC)
- Both parties have a certain stated percentage ownership in the account.
- When one of the parties dies their percentage of the account goes to the deceased estate

Transfer on Death (TOD)
- TOD is a single account that will automatically be transferred to the tenant's estate
- This account might be a good idea if for example you do not like your son-in-law enough to give him part of your net worth before you pass away [just a thought].

Trust Accounts

A trust offers flexibility to an individual who wishes to transfer property. A trust may also be established as a legal entity for a corporate retirement plan

Trust Parties

The Settlor: the person who supplies the property for the trust. The settlor is also known as the maker, grantor, trustor, or donor

Trustee: the holder of property on behalf of another beneficiary. The trustee is a fiduciary and is obligated to perform in the interest of the beneficiaries.

Beneficiary: the person for whom property in a trust is held. The beneficiary may only be the person designated to receive benefits from property transferred by a grantor

If assets placed in a trust is distributed during the year it is received, it is a simple trust. In a complex trust assets are permitted to accumulated income. A complex trust makes distributions of net income or principal.

Living Trusts

A living trust is established during the settlor's lifetime and has complete control over the assets and manages them for the benefit of the beneficiary. A successor is always named and takes over upon the settlor's death. Being able to avoid a probate is a living trust's main advantage

Testamentary Trust

Any trust that comes into being on death through a will is a testamentary trust. The trustee is the legal owner of the property held in the trust and has the authority to control the management of assets. Unlike living trusts, testamentary trust do not avoid probate

Revocable Trust

Since only the settlor can change or revoke the trust, a revocable trust must be a living trust. The trust becomes irrevocable at the settlor's death.

Irrevocable Trust

A trust is irrevocable is the settlor gives up all ownership in property transferred into the trust. Property placed in an irrevocable trust is usually not included in the settlor's estate for federal estate tax. There are some exceptions when property in a trust is included in the settlor's estate:

- If the settlor retains a life interest or life income
- If the settlor may receive property back from the trust (reversionary interest
- If the settlor retains general power to direct to whom trust property will pass
- If the settlor transfers life insurance policies into an ILIT while retaining certain incidents of ownership

Taxation on Trusts

Trusts are taxed based on what is distributed and what is not distributed. Nondistributed income may be subject to the highest tax bracket of 35%.

Distributable Net Income
Most trust distribute their income in order to avoid the high tax on undistributed income. This taxable income is known as distributable net income (DNI). Commissions and other fees involved in buying and selling securities held in the trust are subtracted from DNI. Reinvested capital gains are also not considered part of DNI

Bypass Trust
Bypass trusts are used primarily between spouses. Although one spouse can leave another an unlimited amount of money without incurring a tax, when the surviving spouse dies, the lifetime estate tax exclusion included in the bypass trust help lower the tax liability on the property in the trust. When the second spouse dies, the first $3.5 million passed on to their children is tax free under the unified credit rule

Generation Skipping Trust (GST)
A generation skipping trust is used to pass money to family members more than one generation removed. Using the generation skipping trust, the assets avoid being taxed upon the parents' death and again when their children pass them on to the grandchildren. Similar to a bypass trust, the unified credit rule can be used. Additionally, a GST allow has zero tax liability when the trust is funded with appreciating assets

Estate Accounts

An estate account is a custodial account. Like a trust account it is managed by an executor who makes all the investment, distribution, and management decisions in the account. Taxation in estate accounts are the same as that of trusts.

Recommendations in estate accounts, as with any other account, must be suitable for each estate. Unlike other accounts, the objectives of trust and estate account are clearly stated in the trust document, or the will in the case of an estate, and must be followed. Conflicts between the grantor and the beneficiary may exist

Business Accounts

Sole Proprietorship
A sole proprietorship is the business of an individual business owner and is treated like an individual account. The same suitability issues apply

Partnerships
Partnerships are businesses formed under a partnership agreement. Because partnerships are set up to allow the business' profits and losses to flow directly to investors, in order to avoid double taxation, the objectives of each individual partner must be considered for suitability

Limited Liability Company (LLC)
A LLC combines the benefits of incorporation with the tax advantages of a partnership. The objectives of each individual member of the LLC must be considered for suitability, as in partnerships

S Corporation
An S corporation offers investors the limited liability associated with corporations but is taxed like a partnership. An S corporation can have no more than 100 shareholders, and no shareholder can be a nonresident alien. Losses on S corporation stock may only be claimed to the extent of the money the investor contributed or lent to the corporation

C Corporation
A C corporation distinguishes the company as a separate entity from its owners. The corporation's officers are not liable for losses and debts in most circumstances. Taxes are not passed through to investors like other forms of businesses

Margin Accounts

Margin accounts allow investors to borrow money from their broker dealer to buy securities

Long Margin

Borrow money to buy securities and pay interest until the loan is paid back

Short Margin

- Stocks are borrowed from the broker/dealer, sold, bought back at a lower price and returned to the broker/dealer
- The investor keeps the difference between the two prices

Advantages

For Investor
- Buy stocks with lower cash outlay
- Leverage the position

For broker/dealer
- Receives interest income
- Margin customers typically trades larger positions, which leads to larger commissions

Custodial Accounts

Custodial accounts are opened under the Uniform Gifts to Minors Act (UGMA) or Uniform Transfers to Minors Act (UTMA) which are the regulations that allow minors to have brokerage accounts. The minor is the beneficial owner of the account and is responsible for the taxes.

The minor's SS# is therefore needed to open the account.

The securities in a UGMA or UTMA account are managed by a custodian until the minor reaches the age of majority. The custodian can buy or sell securities, and exercise rights or warrants. The custodian can use property in the account in any way for the minor's support.

The followings are characteristics of custodial accounts
- Custodial accounts can only be opened and managed as cash accounts
- Purchases on margin are prohibited
- Covered call writing is allowed
- Warrants and rights must be exercised or sold
- Dividends, cash proceeds, and interest payments must be reinvested in a reasonable period of time
- Securities must be registered in the donor's name for the benefit of the minor
- In certain states the transfer of UTMA accounts from the donor to the minor can be delayed until the minor reaches age 21 or 25 depending on the state

The minor must file an income tax return every year on a custodial account and pay taxes on any income exceeding $1,900 produced by the account at the parent's top marginal tax rate. Income is taxed at the child's tax rate when the child turns 19, or at 23 if the child is a full-time student

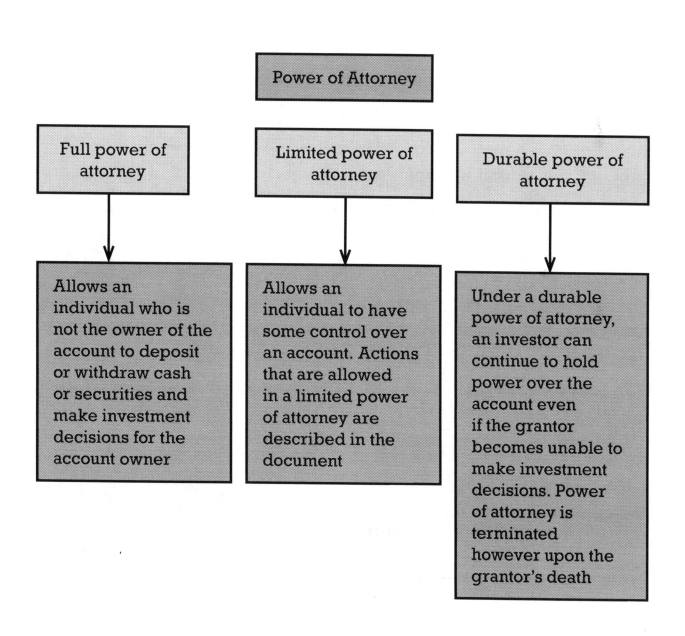

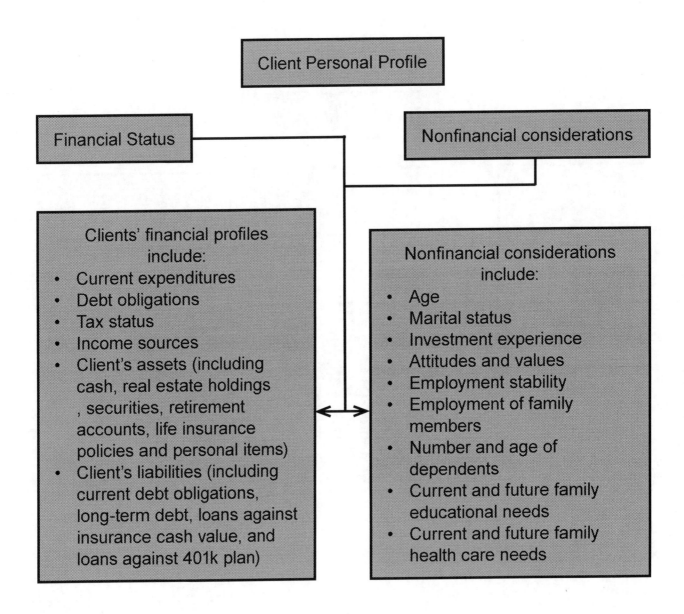

Client Personal Profile

Risk Tolerance

To understand
an investor's risk
tolerance, an adviser
must be aware of the
following:
The liquidity required
for investments
Tax considerations
Losses the investor
can tolerate (5%,
10%, 50% etc)
Investment time
horizon (long-term or
short-term)
Investment
experience
Return expectations
Current holdings
Investment
temperament
Level of tolerance for
market fluctuations

An investor's risk tolerance is his
attitude towards risk and safety.
An investor's risk tolerance should
shape his portfolio no matter what his
financial status

**Aggressive
investors**
Willing to take on
more risks for the
chance to realized
higher rates of return

**Conservative
Investors**
Want safety of stable
income (interest from
bonds or dividends
from stable
companies)

Financial Goals

Death Benefits	Retirement	Disability
Individuals have various opportunities to make sure financial support is in place for their relatives in the event of their passing away. Death benefits should cover a client's mortgage and other debts, income for survivors, college tuition and estate taxes	When determining a client's retirement needs, Social Security, company pension, retirement savings accounts, and insurance should all be considered. A longer time horizon-the longer the individual has before retiring-allows the individual to assume additional risk in an investment portfolio, generally through securities. The earlier an individual starts saving for retirement, the more time the investments have to grow	A client who becomes disabled has three possible income sources: workers' compensation, Social Security and disability insurance. Workers' compensation covers an employee who gets injured on the job. Social Security benefits are based on age and income. A worker can purchase private disability insurance. Most workers are covered under programs supported by employers

Financial Goals

Preservation of Capital

For investors that are averse to any decline in the value of their investments, appropriate investments are CDs, highly rated bonds, savings accounts, and money market funds. Investors who want to avoid risk and preserve capital usually sacrifice the opportunity for higher returns. In addition they are subject to interest rate risk.

Time Horizon

Time horizon refers to how long an investor has before he will need the invested funds and determines the level of volatility the investor can assume. A longer time horizon allows an investor to assume more short-term risk. With a time horizon of less than three years an investor should invest in safe and liquid investments

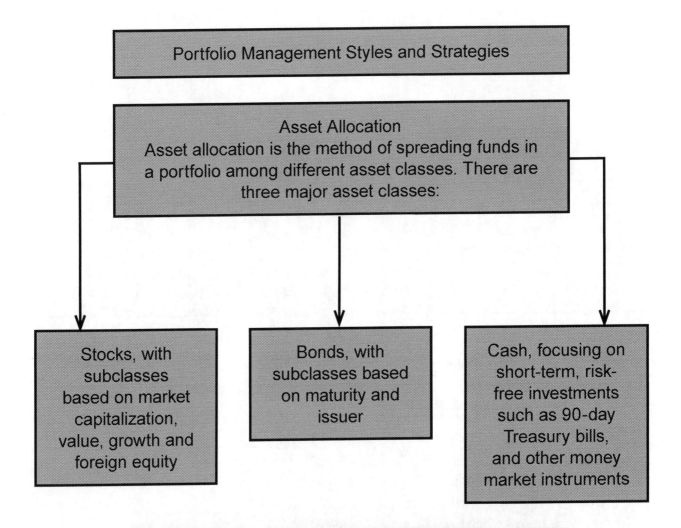

Strategic Asset Allocation

Constant Ratio Plan
A method that seeks to maintain a certain proportion of different asset classes in a long-term portfolio. One method, for example, states by subtracting an investor's age from 100, the amount of the portfolio that should be invested in stocks is determined

Constant Dollar Plan
Under this plan, a constant amount is kept in specific asset classes. For example, if an investor wants to keep $50,000 in stocks and the value of his stock holdings increases to $65,000, $15,000 must be liquidated

Tactical Asset Allocation

Short-term adjustments in a portfolio in consideration of current market conditions.

Sector Rotation
Since different sectors of the economy are stronger depending on the business cycle, some managers try to rotate their holdings to sectors that are expected to move on in the near future. Conversely, when a sector is at its peak, managers would move sell the stocks of those companies

Active

An active management style relies on the manager's ability to pick stocks and time the market. An active manager uses a particular stock selection approach to buy and sell individual stocks

Passive

A passive manager believes no particular management style will outperform the market, therefore he constructs a portfolio that mirrors a market index

Management Styles

Growth

Managers who focus on growth focus on stocks of companies whose earnings are growing faster than most stocks and are expected to continue growing. Growth manager are likely to buy stocks at the high end of their 52-week range

Value

Value oriented managers focus on stocks that are undervalued and out-of-favor. Those stocks' prices are low relative to the companies' earnings and book value. Value investment managers are likely to buy stocks at the bottom of their 52-week range

Current Income

Investors seeking income can invest in fixed income securities such as government bonds and notes, and agency bonds, corporate bonds and notes, preferred stock and utility company stock

Capital Growth

Investors seeking growth are seeking to increase buying power above the inflation rate. An investor with a high tolerance for risk and the ability to remain in the market for years can invest in aggressive growth stocks. Investing in large capitalization stock funds may be more appropriate for investors who are less comfortable with high risk, and older investors.

Diversification

By investing in an array of investment classes, an investor can reduce market risk and enhance returns. The securities in a diversified portfolio are chosen because a security can offset losses from another security-when the price of one security decreases, another one's price increases

Buy and hold

Buy and hold can be used for just about any investment style. A buy and hold manager rarely trades and as a results, incur lower transactions costs and long term capital gains

Dollar-Cost Averaging

Using dollar-cost averaging, investors invest a fixed amount at regular intervals (monthly or quarterly). This strategy allows investors to purchase more shares when prices are low and fewer shares when prices are high. An advantage of dollar-cost averaging is that is helps reduce the effects of timing risk. Additionally, in a fluctuating market, the average cost per share is lower than the average price per share

Taxation

Progressive
Progressive taxes apply to incomes and estate taxes. As income increases, the tax rate increases. A progressive tax system is costlier to high income earners

Regressive
Regressive taxes are levied equally regardless of income and represent a smaller percentage of high earners' income than low earners' income

Corporate Taxes

Dividend exclusion rules: 70% of the dividends received by a corporation from an investment in another corporation are exempt from taxation and pay taxes on only 30% of the dividends received

Municipal securities: like individuals, corporations do not pay taxes on interest received from municipal bonds

Individual Income Taxes

Earned income: earned income is income from direct participation in a trade or business (salaries bonuses)

Alimony and Child Support: Alimony is court ordered payment made to an ex-spouse and child support is a legal obligation of a parent to provide financial support to a child. Alimony is deductible for the person paying it and includable in income by person receiving it. Child support is neither deductible by the person paying nor includable in income by the person receiving it.

Passive income: passive income is income receive from a business where the person is not an active participant (e.g. rental property, limited partnerships, enterprises. Passive income is netted against passive losses to determine net taxable income

Portfolio income: portfolio income includes dividends, interest, and net capital gains from the sale of securities. Portfolio income is taxed in the year in which it is received

Alternative Minimum Tax (AMT)

The alternative minimum tax was enacted by congress to ensure that high-income earners do not avoid paying federal income taxes. Under AMT, certain items must be added back to taxable income, which includes:

- Accelerated depreciation on property placed in service after 1986
- Local tax and interest on investments that do not generate income
- Employee stock options to the extent that the fair market value of the stock exceeds the strike price
- Tax-exempt interest on private purpose municipal bonds issued after August 7, 1986
- Certain costs of limited partnership programs, such as research and development costs and excess intangible drilling costs

Taxes on Capital Gains and Losses

Net Capital Gains

To calculate tax liability, capital losses must be subtracted from capital gains to arrive at net capital gains or losses. This allows investors to offset capital gains with capital losses. Short-term gains (gains from securities held for less than 12 months) are taxed at the investor's ordinary income tax rate. Long-term capital gains (securities held for more than 12 months) are taxed at 15%. Investors can deduct up to $3,000 in net capital losses against earned income. Losses not deducted in the current year can be carried forward indefinitely in future years

Adjusting Cost Basis

When a security is sold, the result of that sale can be a capital gain or capital loss. An investment's cost basis-the cost of making an investment-is used to calculate if the sale of an investment resulted in a capital gain or loss.

Estate and Gift Taxes

Estate Tax

Gift tax

Estate taxes are imposed on the transfer of large amounts of property upon death. A transfer of property to a spouse, no matter what the amount, is not subject to an estate tax. An individual can also transfer funds to an eligible charity without incurring an estate tax

A transfer of property made during the lifetime of the donor is taxed as a gift. Up to $1 million in lifetime gifts can be made without incurring gift tax. An individual can also give up to $13,000 per year to any number of individuals without incurring a gift tax. A gift to a spouse who is not a citizen is subject to gift tax

To arrive at the actual taxable estate, we begin with gross estate, which includes all interest in property held by the individual at the time of death. Certain deduction, such as funeral costs and debts, are made to arrive at adjusted gross estate. From adjusted gross estate, transfers to a spouse and an eligible charity, are subtracted to arrive at the taxable estate

Individual Retirement Accounts (IRA)

Created to encourage people to save for retirement in addition to other plans

Contributions
Contributions of the lesser of $5,000 or 100% of income are allowed
Contributions must by made by April 15 for the previous tax year
Contributions are tax-deductible if the individual does not qualify for any other qualified plans
Municipal securities are not appropriate for IRAs
No short sales or margin trading are allowed in IRAs

Distributions
May begin after age 59 ½ without a penalty
Distributions before age 59 ½ are penalized at 10% and taxed as ordinary income
Distributions must begin by April 1 in the year after the individual turns 70 ½

An IRA can be rolled-over only once a year

Roth IRAs allow after-tax contributions up to a maximum annual allowance

Individual Retirement Accounts

Compensation for IRA Purposes

Compensation:

- Wages, salaries and tips
- Commissions
- Self-employment income
- Alimony
- Nontaxable combat pay

Not compensation:

- Capital gains
- Interest and dividend income
- Pension or annuity income
- Child support
- Passive income from DPPs

Roth IRA

Unlike traditional IRAs, contributions to Roth IRAs are not deductible. As a result, contributions may be withdrawn tax-free. Gains in the account are withdrawn tax-free after five years if :

- The account holder is 59½ or older
- The money is used for the first-time purchase of a principal residence
- The account holder has died or become disabled
- The money is used to pay for qualified higher education expenses
- The money is paid to pay for certain medical expenses or medical insurance premiums

Contributions

Contribution limits are the same as for traditional IRAs. Unlike traditional IRAs contributions can be made past age 70½, as long as the account holder has earned income.

Eligibility

Anyone with earned income is eligible to open a Roth IRA provided their gross income is below a certain level. The full contribution amount can be made if the if the individual's gross income is below $105,000 per year. The ability to contribute the full amount is phased out between $105,000 and $120,000. For married couples filing job returns, the limit is $166,000

Retirement Plans

Qualified	Nonqualified
Contributions tax-deductible	Contributions not tax-deductible
Needs IRS approval	Does not need IRS approval
Cannot discriminate	Can discriminate
Tax on accumulation is deferred	Tax on accumulation is deferred
All withdrawals are taxed	Withdrawals in excess of total contributions are tax
Plan is a trust	Plan is not a trust

Two types of Nonqualified plans

Deferred compensation: agreement between a company and employee in which the employee agrees to defer the receipt of current income in favor of payout at retirement

Payroll deduction: allows employees to authorize their employer to deduct a specified amount for retirement from their paychecks. The money is deducted after taxes

Profit-Sharing Plans

A profit-sharing plan allows an employer to participate in the business's profits. Payments may be made directly to the employees or paid into an account for future payment. Profit-sharing plans do not need to have a predetermined contribution formula. Plans that do use such a formula generally express contributions as a percentage of profits. Employers are also allowed to skip contributions in years of low profits

401(k) Plans

401(k) plans allow employees to direct an employer to contribute a percentage of his salary to a retirement account. Employers also have the opportunity to match employee contributions to a 401(k) plan. All contributions are made with pretax dollars.

401(k) Plan Loans
Unlike hardship withdrawals, 401(k) plan loans are not taxed if the meet certain IRS guidelines. Loans have a maximum of the lesser of $50,000 or the employees vested share. All loans must carry a "reasonable rate of interest" according to the IRS

Hardship Withdrawals

Hardship withdrawals are permitted when a participant is facing immediate and serious financial difficulty. Withdrawals are taxed at ordinary income and may be subject to a 10% penalty

Roth 401(k) Plans
Roth 401(k) contributions are made with after-tax dollars and withdrawals are tax free as long as they are made at age 59½ or older. Employer contributions must be made into a regular 401(k) and be fully taxable at withdrawal. Although that would mean the employee has two accounts, he would not be able to transfer money between the two accounts

Self-Employed 401(k) Plans
The purpose of self-employed 401(k) plans is to allow sole proprietorships to set up and contribute to a 401(k) plan. In order to contribute to a 401(k) plan, the business owner may not have any full-time employees other than himself and his spouse. Withdrawal rules are the same as for traditional IRAs

403 (b) Plans

403(b) plans were created for employees of public school systems, and tax-exempt, non-profit organizations, such as churches and charitable organization. Maximum contributions to 403(b) plans is the lesser of 100% of income or $49,000 per year

Tax Advantages

Income Inclusion
Contributions to a 403(b) plan can be excluded from taxable income, as long as they do not exceed the maximum limit

Tax-Deferred Accumulation
Earnings in a 403(b) plan accumulate without incurring taxes. Participants do pay taxes at withdrawal

Section 457 Plan

Section 457 plans were set up for employees of a state, political subdivision of a state, any agency instrumentality of a state, or certain tax-exempt organizations

Section 457 Plan Characteristics
Exempt from ERISA
Generally not required to follow nondiscriminatory rules of other retirement plans
Plans for tax-exempt organizations only cover high income employees
Distributions may not be rolled over into an IRA
There is no 10% penalty for early withdrawal
No loans are permitted to be taken from 457 plans
Holding a 457 plan and a 403(b) plan and making the maximum contribution to both is allowed

Employee Retirement Income Security Act of 1974 (ERISA)

Employee Retirement Income Security Act of 1974 (ERISA)
- Established to prevent abuse and misuse of pension funds
- Employees must be covered is over age 21 with one or more continuous years of full time services (1,000 hours)
- Retirement funds separate from corporate assets
- Employees are entitled to their entire benefit
- Annual statements required
- All eligible employees must be impartially treated through uniformly applied formula
- Beneficiaries must be named to receive benefits at employees death

ERISA provides the guidelines for the regulations of retirement plans, which include the following:

- Employers must cover their employers if they offer a retirement plan and if the employee is aged 21 or older, have one year of service, and work 1,000 hours per year
- Funds contributed to the retirement plan must be set apart from other corporate assets. The plan's trustees have a responsibility to invest and manage funds in a way that is in the best interest of the employees
- Within a certain amount of time, employees must be entitled to their benefits even if they no longer work for the company
- The plan must be in writing, and employees must be kept informed of different of the plan at least annually
- The plan must have a uniformly applied formula to determine contribution and benefits

Fiduciary Responsibility Under ERISA

Fiduciaries must act:

- Solely in the interest of the plan participants and beneficiaries
- Only for the purpose of providing benefits to participants and their beneficiaries and defraying reasonable expenses
- With the care, skill, prudence, and diligence that a prudent professional would use
- To diversify investments to minimize the risk of large losses, unless doing so is clearly not prudent under the circumstances
- In accordance with the governing plan documents unless they are not in compliance with ERISA

Investment Policy Statement

ERISA does not require an investment policy statement. However it is suggested that each employee benefit plan have an investment policy statement in writing as a guideline for the fiduciary follow when making decisions regarding funding and management

Prohibited Transactions
A fiduciary is prohibited from engaging in the following under ERISA:

- Dealing with plan assets for his own benefit
- Acting in a transaction involving the plan for a party that has different interests from the plan
- Receiving compensation for his personal account from any party dealing with the plan in connection with plan transactions

Keogh Plan

Keogh Plans are qualified plans for self-employed and owner-employees of unincorporated business

Eligibility

The following are eligible to participate in a Keogh plan:
Employees who receive compensation for at least 1,000 hours of work per year
Employees who have completed one or more years of continuous employment
Employees who are 21 years and older

Contributions

Up to $49,000 may be contributed on behalf of a Keogh plan participant in a year. Participants are also eligible for an IRA. Participants can also make after-tax contributions to a Keogh plan, however total contributions (pre-tax and after-tax) cannot exceed the maximum limit

Coverdell Education Savings Account

Coverdell ESAs allow after-tax (non-deductible) contributions ($2,000 per beneficiary) for student beneficiaries. Those contributions must be made in cash and before the beneficiary turns 18 unless the beneficiary is a "special needs beneficiary". Accumulation in a Coverdell ESA are tax-deferred and when distributed, the earnings portion is excluded from income when it is used to pay qualified education expenses. Distributions that are not used for qualified education expenses are taxed and incur an additional 10% penalty.

Section 529 Plans

Known as qualified tuition plans, 529 plans are state-operated investment plans that give families a way to save money for college with substantial tax benefits

Prepaid Tuition Plans
Prepaid tuitions plans allow college savers to pay for tuition at participating colleges and universities (room and board in some cases). Prepaid tuition plans are generally sponsored by state governments and have residency requirements. Prepaid tuition plans lock in today's tuition rate

College Savings Plans
In college savings plans, the contributor, or account holder, establishes an account for a student (beneficiary) in order to pay for the student's qualified college expenses. Withdrawals can be used at any college or university

Contributions and Taxes

Contributions in a 529 plan can be a lump sum or periodic payments. Contributions are made with after-tax dollars and distributions are exempt from federal taxes and state taxes in most cases. Distributions that are not used for qualified education expenses are subject to income tax and a 10% penalty

---

Unused funds can be can be rolled over to a member the beneficiary's family without incurring taxes. However the rollover must be completed within 60 days of the distribution. Immediate family members include:

- Son, daughter, stepchild, foster child, adopted child or a descendant of any of them
- Brother, sister, step brother, or step sister
- Father or mother or ancestor of either
- Stepfather or stepmother
- Son or daughter of a brother or sister
- Brother or sister of father or mother
- Son-in-law, daughter-in-law, father-in-law, mother-in-law, brother-in-law, or sister in law
- The spouse of any of the above
- First cousin

Quantitative Measures of Investment Risks

Time Value of Money

How should I invest today to get $100 ten years from now?
To answer this question it is important to understand the "time value of money"

The time value of money is the difference between its present value (its value today) and its future value. If an investor can earn 10% compounded annually, using the example above, the investor would have to invest $38.55 today

Future Value
The formal term used to indicate what an amount invested today, at a given rate, will be worth in the future is called future value
The formula used to calculate the future value of money invested today is as follows

$$FV = PV \times (1 + r)^{10}$$
$$FV = 38.55 \times (1 + .10)^{10}$$

FV = Future Value
PV = Present Value
r = rate of return

t = time period over which the money is invested

Present Value

Present value is the value today of the future cash flows of an investment discounted at a specified interest rate. To determined the present worth of those future cash flows, use the following formula

$$PV = FV \div (1 + r)^t$$

Rule of 72

The rule of 72 is a shortcut used to determine how long it will take for an investment to double in value. By dividing 72 by the interest rate paid by the investment, or the yearly rate of return of the investment, you arrive at the number of years it will take for the investment to double. For example, an investment returning 8% per year, will double in approximately 9 years (72 ÷ 8 = 9)

Investment Return Measurements

Total return: the income (interest or dividend) plus growth of principal from an investment

Current yield
(stock)
Annual dividend payout

Market value per common share

(bond)
Annual interest

Current market price

Yield to Maturity (Basis)

Yield to Maturity measures the gain or loss from an investment in a bond if the bond is held to maturity

Holding period return: the total return received on an investment during the period it was held

Annualized return: the return on an investment if it was held for one year. The annualized return is calculated by multiplying the actual return by the annualization factor (the number of days in the year divided by the number of days the investment was held

After-tax return: the return on an investment after tax is paid
Inflation-adjusted return (real return): inflation-adjusted return is a measure of the buying power earned from an investment. The inflation-adjusted return can be calculated by subtracting the nominal return of an investment by a benchmark index such as the consumer price index (CPI)

Expected return: estimated returns that an investment may yield

Net present value: the difference between an investment's present value and its cost

Internal rate of return (IRR): the discount rate that makes the future value of an investment equal to its present value. A bond's yield to maturity is its IRR. IRR is not practical for common stock because of uneven cash flow and lack of maturity date and price

IRR calculations

Time-weighted returns: calculates IRR by evaluating the performance of a portfolio manager without the influence of new investor deposits or withdrawals in the portfolio

Dollar-weighted returns: IRR earned on the basis of the investor's clash flow into and out of the portfolio

These two methods will show very different results when used to calculate investment returns. Investors who wish to calculate the return in their portfolio will primarily use the dollar-weighted method since that method shows the true return on every dollar invested. However, the time-weighted is more appropriate to use when evaluating a portfolio manager since that method shows the portfolio manager's performance without the effect of money being added to or withdrawn from the portfolio

Dividend Models

Dividend discount model

This model states the value of a stock should be equal to the present value of all future dividends. To find the value of a stock, divide the expected future dividends by the required rate of return

Dividend growth model

This model expects annual dividends to grow at a constant rate. This model is best when used with other forecasting tools

Dividend models are used by analysts who believe the value of a stock can be determined based on current of future dividends. Since bigger and well established companies tend to pay regular dividends, dividend models are best used to value the stock of those companies

Financial Ratios

Current ratio: a measure of a company's ability to meet its short-term obligations. The higher the ratio the more liquid the company is

$$\text{Current ratio} = \frac{\text{Current assets}}{\text{Current liabilities}}$$

Quick ratio (acid test ratio): a stricter test of a company's ability to meet its short-term obligations

$$\text{Quick ratio} = \frac{\text{Current assets} - \text{inventory}}{\text{Current liabilities}}$$

Debt to equity ratio: a measure of a company's financial leverage

$$\text{Debt-to-equity} = \frac{\text{Total liability}}{\text{Total shareholders equity}}$$

Book value per share: the liquidation value of a company (the money left if the company sold all its assets and paid all its debt)

$$\text{Book value per share} = \frac{\text{Net tangible assets} - \text{liabilities} - \text{par value of preferred stock}}{\text{Number of shares of common stock outstanding}}$$

Corporate SEC Filings

Form 8-K: this form is filed with the SEC to report newsworthy events such as mergers and acquisitions, change in management, change in company name, bankruptcy filings, and the introduction or sale of a new product

Form 10-K: this form is an annual report and overview of a company's business and financial condition. It includes a financial statements (balance sheet, income statement, and cash flow statement) audited by an independent accountant

Form 10-Q: this form is a quarterly report of a company's financial conditions. The 10-Q is not audited, unlike the 10-K, and is not filed after the fourth quarter

Annual report: this report contains a company's financial condition, future plans and voting proxies. It is less detailed than the 10-K

Prospectus: the prospectus is a summarized version of the registration statement. It contains all the material facts needed for an investor to make an informed investment decision. Every person solicited for the sale of a security must receive a copy of the prospectus

Risk Measurements

Risk is defined as the uncertainty that an investment will earn its expected return.
Risk is also referred to as volatility.

Beta (or beta coefficient): a measure of a stock's volatility in relation to the overall market. A beta of 1 means the stock moves in line with the market. A stock with a beta is higher than 1 is a stock that is more volatile than the market. A stock with a beta less than 1 is a stock less volatile than the market. A high beta suggest high capital gains in a rising market, and greater losses in a falling market

Standard deviation: a measure of volatility of an investment's projected returns. The higher the standard deviation the more an investment's returns are expected to deviate from its average return, thus, the greater the risk

Monte Carlo simulations: computer generated estimated returns. MCSs are used to address problems with unknown variables, address situations where no real-world date exists, and to address problems for which no analytical solution exists

Investment Risk

Investment risk is divided in two categories:
Systematic and Unsystematic.

Systematic risks are:
- Market risk
- Interest rate risk
- Inflation or purchasing power risk

Unsystematic risks are:
- Business risk
- Liquidity risk
- Political risk
- Regulatory risk

Business Risk

The risk that the business fails. When a business fails and is liquidated, the company's stock often becomes worthless, resulting in a capital loss for the investor

Market Risk

The risk that changes in the overall market will have an adverse effect on individual stocks regardless of the company's circumstances

Interest Rate Risk

Fluctuations in interest rate affect bond prices. The Federal Reserve can decide to raise or lower rates, can lower or increase bond prices respectively

Regulatory Risk

Sudden and major changes in regulations can have a negative effect on businesses

Inflation Risk (Purchasing Power Risk)

In a growing economy, a modest level of inflation is healthy. However a high rate of inflation decrease the value of the dollar and its purchasing power

Legislative Risk

The difference between regulatory risk and legislative risk is that regulatory risk comes from changes in regulations whereas legislative, or political, risk comes from changes in the law

Liquidity Risk

The ease of being able to sell a security and convert it into cash

Opportunity Cost

The highest valued investment that must be sacrificed to in order to invest in another opportunity

Reinvestment Risk

The risk that a periodic cash flow from an investment may not be invested at the same or higher rate

Currency or Exchange Risk

That risk that currency rates will fluctuate and lead to change in investment growth or loss solely due to currency fluctuations (this applies to foreign investments)

Asset Classes

Cash and cash equivalents: savings and checking accounts, T-bills, money market accounts, money market funds and certificates of deposits

Fixed – income investment: corporate bonds, municipal bonds, Treasury bonds, bond funds and mortgage backed securities

Equities – common and preferred stock

Hard assets – real estate, collectibles, precious metals and stones

The above asset classes each responds different to different types of risks. By diversifying investments among those asset classes, investors can reduce volatility and risk overall, and improve portfolio performance

Benchmark portfolios

Standard and Poor's 500

The S&P 500 Composite Index is made up of four main groups of securities: 400 industrials, 20 transportation companies, 40 public utility companies, and 40 financial institutions. Most of the stock in the S&P 500 are listed on the NYSE. Some are also listed on the AMEX, and the Nasdaq. The S&P is a cap-weighted index

NYSE Index

The NYSE publishes a composite index that includes all 3,000 companies listed on the exchange. The index provides the most comprehensive measure of activity on the NYSE. The NYSE index is also cap-weighted

Nasdaq Composite Index

The Nasdaq Composite Index is an index of the over-the-counter market and covers more than 3,000 over-the-counter companies. This index is also cap-weighted

Dow Jones Industrial Average

The DJIA is published by Dow Jones & Company (publisher of the Wall Street Journal). The DJIA is made up of 30 of the most well-known corporations in the world. Unlike the S&P 500 and the NYSE index, the DJIA is price-weighted.

Efficient Market Hypothesis

The efficient market hypothesis (EMH) states that stock prices always reflect all available information and are efficiently priced. This theory is also referred to as the random walk theory. This theory is basically stating that throwing a dart at the stock listings is as good as any other stock picking method.

Versions of EMH

Weak	Semi-strong	Strong
This version of EMH suggest that all past information about a stock is reflected in its price. According to EMH, having all this information should not enable anyone to beat the market because it is information everyone knows	In addition toe past information, the semi-strong form of EMH includes information reported in a company's financial statements, announcements and economic factors	Insider information is included in the strong form of EMH. Under the strong form, public and private information is reflected in the stock price. The belief is that the market is an anticipatory vehicle and moves based on anticipated developments

Modern Portfolio Theory

Modern portfolio theory attempts to measure and control portfolio risk. It puts an emphasis on determining the relationship between risk and reward, and the relationship among all the investments in the portfolio as a whole instead of individual securities. This is derived from the capital asset pricing model, which states that an investor should be rewarded for risks taken, thus the higher the risk, the higher the expected return. To reduce risk, modern portfolio theory uses diversification. Diversification only reduces risk when assets in the portfolio move inversely or at different times.

Capital Market Line

Capital market line provides an expected return based on the level of risk by using the portfolio's expected return, the risk free rate, the return on the market, the standard deviation of the market, and the standard deviation of the market

Security Market Line

The security market line provides an expected return of individual securities by using the expected return of the security, the risk-free rate, the return on the market, and the beta of the security

$$5\% + 1(15\% - 5\%) = 5\% + 1(10\%) = 5\% + 10\% = 15\%$$

risk-free return   beta   market expected return   expected return of security